Among Others

Among Others

Friendships and Encounters

MICHAEL FRAYN

faber

First published in 2023
by Faber & Faber Limited
Bloomsbury House
74–77 Great Russell Street
London WC1B 3DA

Typeset by Faber & Faber Limited
Printed in England by CPI Group (UK) Ltd, Croydon, CRO 4YY

A CIP record for this book
is available from the British Library

ISBN 978–0–571–37860–9

Printed and bound in the UK on FSC paper in line with our continuing
commitment to ethical business practices, sustainability and the environment.
For further information see faber.co.uk/environmental-policy

2 4 6 8 10 9 7 5 3 1

Contents

Among Others

Makers

You are what you eat. Not just the food on your plate that you take in through your mouth and digest with your stomach – the whole world around you that you take in through your eyes and ears and digest with your brain. What would you be without it? Contentless. A camera with an unexposed film. A set of possibilities framed by your genetic inheritance, but never realised. A something unshaped and unformed. A nothing.

You might make an environment out of very little. An orphan cast away at birth on a desert island would no doubt construct a self of some kind out of the wind and the surf, the bare rocks and the seabirds. How much richer and more formative his surroundings would become, though, when Man Friday arrives. More than anything else, surely, it's the other human beings in our lives who make us who we are.

Each of them, for a start, is a life-size model of oneself, a picture of how one appears to the outside world. Which is striking enough. But the second most noticeable thing about them is that they are *not* oneself – not pictures or reflections. They are totally different – genetically different sets of possibilities, each shaped by a different environment. One of the things that makes that environment different is that it contains a different selection of other people. Each of whom has been shaped by yet another environment and another selection of people that they in their turn have to deal with.

There's something slightly comic about this in my case. One of the things that preoccupied me when I was a child was trying to make a man. Or at least a dummy. Over and over again on wet afternoons I would lay out clothes on the floor and fill them with cushions and towels, then make a head out of a pair of underpants stuffed with socks and put a papier-mâché mask on the front of it. This is more or less how I have spent a lot of my professional life since, of course, making men and women, but out of words and sentences instead of cushions and socks. And all the time, I realise now I look back on it, I was being moulded into shape myself by the people around me.

I started thinking, late in life, about all these people I have come into contact with in the past eighty years or so, and who have made me what I am, for better or for worse, and this life of mine what it has been. Some have had a profound effect, some a small and passing one. Some have had no real effect that I'm conscious of, but remain part of my mental fabric because my recollection of them is for some reason so vivid.

It was my parents, of course, who shaped the beginnings of my life, and I've written about them at some length already. In fact I've devoted a whole book to them, which also contains an account of the friend who had the most powerful effect on my adolescence, and two of my schoolteachers. But what about all the people who have composed my world since? All the tutors and lecturers who have taught me, all my fellow students who gave me such intriguing glimpses into their own subjects – architecture in particular, psychology, anthropology? Then there are the colleagues I have worked with – the editors who have improved my books, the producers, directors and actors who have brought my plays to life. And all the other people I have had dealings with, who made me see things their way or react against it, who coloured the bald outlines of the world around me right or wrong, serious or ridiculous, agreeable or disagreeable. I seem to be a particularly influenceable subject – a natural lieutenant, always ready to follow people who are by nature leaders, always eager to be diverted by passing attractions.

So I should like to say a brief word about a few of these people who have made my world, and me with it, before my memory finally goes. I owe so much to so many of them – and there's so little that I can remember doing for them in return. What follows isn't intended as biographies of them, comprehensive accounts of their lives for the historical record, nor as they see themselves – just a few impressions of my own passing contacts with them, as fleeting as snapshots. I showed the results to the ones who are still alive, and to the surviving relatives of those who aren't. I've incurred even more debts all round for the tolerance and generosity of their responses and for the many suggestions and corrections they've made.

My choice out of all the possible candidates is pretty capricious. One or two of my closest and most enduring friends, certainly; but not others, more or less equally close and enduring. One or two people who left traces of themselves in the fictitious characters I invented professionally. One or two simply because the memory of them amused me. One or two for no good reason at all.

There's one aspect of the selection that seems not so much capricious as weird: there are almost no women in it. I should have expected some sort of disparity, because there were relatively few women in the sexually segregated world in which I grew up. An all-boys school followed by all-male military service. A university with, in those days, nine men to every one woman. A job in a newspaper reporter's room where all my colleagues but one were men. The wonder, now I look back on it, is that I ever came into contact with any women at all.

But of course I did, in spite of everything. My first girlfriend makes her appearance in the memoir of my parents, and so does my first wife. That tiny minority of women students at Cambridge, isolated like another species in just two out of the twenty-four colleges, had a powerful impact on me – no doubt in part precisely because of their rarity. Some of the women that I did get to know marked my life at least as much as any of the men. My three daughters, for instance – but you can't write about your own children! My second wife – but you can't write about your own wife!

Even with all the others, it seems to me, there's often a difficulty. A difference in gender is like a difference in electrical polarity. Not so, I know, for a lot of people, but I don't think I can ever quite escape an awareness of that difference – always intriguing, however faint. The more likely the relationship is to have an effect on you the less likely it is to resemble an ordinary friendship, and the more likely that slight intriguing tingle is to resemble the force that arcs between two thunderclouds. Ordinary friendships are open and you can tell the world about them – past friendships, present friendships. At the heart of a love affair, though, is surely something that can't be made public – while to talk about it without giving any account of that something seems an even worse betrayal. Then again a love affair is exclusive; former lovers, or their later partners, may not want to hear so much as any reference made to the feelings of the past. You can have many friendships at the same time and they can run on for years, become closer or more remote, be forgotten and renewed, fade quietly away. More than one love affair at a time and there's trouble – and that single relationship either develops into a bond that ends only in death, or is broken off short in one painful way or another.

So, it's really only half a world I'm describing, and half I'm remaining awkwardly mute about. I've included just one woman from among my teachers, and one with whom my relationship survived and evolved to become a friendship, or so I thought, though in view of what happened later perhaps I was deceiving myself. I showed an earlier draft of this introduction to Claire, my wife, who has some particular authority in the matter, partly because she is who she is in my life, partly because she is a biographer by trade herself, and one who has managed to write perfectly well in her own memoirs about the men as well as the women in her life – including me. She found my explanation as baffling as what I was trying to explain. So I thought about it again and in the end added at any rate one piece in which I made an attempt to overcome my inhibition.

One of the men I've included is perhaps the closest acquaintance of all – myself. Considered not as a person, though, but as a physical object. Your own body, after all, plays a leading part in the show of which it's also the audience. It's not only the instrument of your consciousness, it's the source of a lot of what you're conscious of – pains and pleasures, information about its disposition in space, its approach to action and its understanding of the results – the ever-present background to your waking world. You take it pretty much for granted – at any rate until something goes wrong – but it's a part of the environment at least as important in making you what you are as the people and things around you. So, among all those others in my life, a word about the world's most endangered species, its only extant non-other.

Stranger on the Hearth

I opened my eyes and found a strange young man standing in front of my fireplace – a slim, elegant figure with a distinctive aureole of golden hair who seemed to have materialised as magically as an angel in a story, and to be as perfectly at home on my hearth. I knew at once who it was, even though I had never set eyes on him before. This was in Cambridge in, I think, the autumn of 1955, and my visitant was the most famous undergraduate in the university, the man everyone wanted to meet. It was my first sight of Bamber Gascoigne, and the start of a friendship that would last for the next sixty years.

He seemed to be amused at my confusion. 'Aren't you coming to your own party?' he said.

My party . . . ? Oh, my party – yes! I was giving it with a friend of mine in the same college as Bamber, and I had been looking forward to it most particularly because my co-host had invited him. But after we had set everything out I had evidently felt so exhausted by all that drawing of corks and polishing of glasses that I had gone back to my own room to have a brief preparatory nap. And failed to wake up. Bamber had probably been enjoying the party, since he was naturally sociable and had a talent for enjoying more or less everything he did. It was entirely characteristic of his sweetness of nature, though – and perhaps also of his curiosity about what kind of person it was who threw a party and then failed to turn up for it – that it was he who had volunteered to leave it and walk all the way across Cambridge to fetch me.

It was inevitable, now that I had met him, that I should be immediately captivated by his charm. Everyone was, then and ever after.
Actually it was something more elusive and more precious than
charm; it was grace. That golden aureole of his seemed to be lit by
a radiance that emanated from himself, and a little of it spilled over
on to everyone he met. He infected us all with his pleasure in life.
He made you feel that *you* were giving *him* pleasure – that you were
the very person he had been hoping at that very moment to meet. It
took a little time, though, to discover what was concealed beneath
that golden surface – a heart no less golden.

I learned so much from him over the years – or tried to. Whenever
I have been uncertain how to behave, socially or morally, I have
found myself, without any conscious decision, wondering what
Bamber would do. Though not always then managing to do it.

I was in my second year at Cambridge when we met, he in his
first. What had made him so famous? As I recalled it when I started
on this piece, it was because of a revue he had written. But a little
research among ancient engagement diaries showed me to my surprise that the revue came a year later. He was famous already. How?
Why? I don't know. He just was. Was and always had been. He certainly had been at school, which is why his arrival in Cambridge had
been anticipated and reported upon. The revue, *Share My Lettuce*,
made him a lot more famous still. Revue was a long-standing tradition at Cambridge; the Footlights May Week show transferred to
the West End for a couple of weeks each summer and kept the entertainment industry supplied with new talent. The show that Bamber
wrote (and directed) was intended more modestly for an audience
in his own college, Magdalene (opening number: 'Dagdalene in

14

Magdalene'), and done with a scratch cast from the college (my friend and fellow party-giver, Michael Collings, among them), but it was performed in the professionally equipped theatre of the university's Amateur Dramatic Club, and, as people in the business used to say, it took the town.

Like its creator, it had charm – a modest, light-hearted, sweet-natured freshness that simply caught people's fancy. Years later, an immensely successful advertising man who had once acted in undergraduate productions told me sadly, 'You're never as famous as you are at Cambridge.' And now this magic spotlight had fallen on someone who was famous already. He was in demand as never before.

A young London theatre producer who was struggling to get a footing in the business, Michael Codron, came to see the show, was captivated, and put it on in the West End, with two stars, Maggie Smith and Kenneth Williams. Much later, when Michael had become the most adventurous and successful producer in London, he told me that *Share My Lettuce* had been make or break for him. His wealthy father had allowed him to have a shot at producing, and every show he had done had failed. If *Share My Lettuce* had gone down in its turn he would have had to retreat into the family textile business. It did succeed, handsomely; it ran not for two weeks, like the Footlights, but for a year or so. One of the beneficiaries of its success, apart from Michael and his investors, was me. In the long term because Michael went on to produce twelve of my plays. There and then as well, because, needing to replace a couple of sketches during the out-of-town try-out, Bamber had generously included one from the less-than-successful Footlights May Week show that I had written later (the first for many years not to get its fortnight

15

in the West End). Which gave me some private satisfaction – and also one thirty-second of the author's royalty. My first earnings in the theatre, and a welcome supplement to the twelve guineas a week I was getting at the time as a reporter on the *Manchester Guardian*.

• • •

Bamber's story, particularly in those early years at Cambridge, raises a number of questions about the psychologically and morally elusive concepts of charm and success. Also, of course, of privilege. Underlying all the pleasure I took in my years at Cambridge, I have to confess, was an awareness of my own privilege in being there. There was a positive side to this – a justifiable gratitude for the huge good fortune I had been granted. There was also, I see, a rather more dubious aspect – an enjoyment of finding myself in a more socially elevated world than the one in which I had been brought up. Some grammar-school boys like myself have claimed to have felt stranded and humiliated by being plunged into what was still a largely public-school world. I really don't think I did. I was intrigued and impressed. I couldn't help admiring the style and self-confidence that so many of my fellow undergraduates had learned from their expensive but harsher upbringing.

Particularly the old Etonians. The ones I met seemed to have a characteristic combination of ability, modesty and style that set them apart. Far from making you feel inferior, they all quite naturally took it upon themselves to put you at your ease, to treat you as an equal, and to make sure you felt that they took as much interest in you as you did in them.

16

Bamber was only one of the number I got to know. I evidently boasted about this with embarrassing naivety to Alan Bennett, a grammar-school boy like myself, with whom I had become friends while we were being trained as Russian interpreters together during our national service, the two years that in those days young men had to spend in the armed services. He had gone on to Oxford, where he was now having as wretched a time in miserable obscurity as I was an agreeable one with my new friends at Cambridge. We maintained a copious correspondence, a good deal of which on his side (idiosyncratically and wittily illustrated) is taken up with savagely funny ridicule of my social aspirations that makes me laugh still – and wince – when I re-read it. I wish I could quote from it here, mortifying though it would be, but I don't think he would allow it. When, many years later, I had a sumptuous colour copy made of it as a birthday present for him, he told me that if it had been the original he would have burned it. A lesson here in the importance of protecting manuscripts from their own authors – and also in the volatility of the success and failure we were all so concerned with, because four short years later he shot into the firmament himself with *Beyond the Fringe* and left us all behind, old Etonians and their admirers alike.

The traffic was not entirely one way. Bamber told me later that he and his friends had been as intrigued to meet people from outside their own little world as we had been to meet them. And our rapprochement was not ephemeral. Not only Bamber but two other Collegers from his year group at Eton, William Plowden and Nicholas Monck, became close friends and remained so for life. The better I got to know them over the years the more impressive they seemed, and the more warmly I felt about them. One of the

qualities they shared, I realise now I think about them as a group
– and a curious one, seeing how many of the old Etonians who
are nowadays prominent in political and business life seem to be
charlatans, thieves and liars – is that they were all genuinely, deeply
good people.

All privilege and advantage are relative, of course, and I came to
understand that the Etonians I was getting to know were mostly
members of a subdivision of the group who had been in somewhat
the same position at school as I was at Cambridge. They were a kind
of grammar-school boys themselves. Eton, like Winchester – like
Cambridge, for that matter – had been founded to educate the sons
not of the affluent but of the clerical classes. Over the centuries
enterprising schoolmasters had set up satellite establishments, the
so-called Oppidan (town) houses, around the central core, so that
the wealthy could buy into the brand, rather as they buy into pic-
turesquely impoverished villages and artists' quarters and destroy
them in the process. But the original heart of Eton had survived,
more or less, and kept its name: College. To get into College you
certainly had to have parents able to pay the fees, and to have put
you through a private preparatory school, so it was still very far
from being what the term 'public school' might seem to suggest.
It was much more exclusive than the other houses, in fact, because
you also had to sit a nationwide competitive exam, and the competition was intense. If you got in you could reasonably suppose that
you were among the very cleverest few hundred privately educated
boys in the country.

The attitude of English philistines, high and low, to cleverness
being what it is, these super-bright Collegers were looked down
upon by the Oppidans, their less clever schoolmates. All this was

part of the lore that I was beginning to learn from my new Colleger friends, and I was fascinated by this insight into a closed world that was so far from my own experience. Collegers were known as tugs, and it was thought correct social usage, so William explained to me, for Oppidans to spit at them and say, 'Dirty little tug, you don't wash.' Bamber told me about a wealthy family he knew whose clever son had won a place in College, but who had felt unable to inflict such humiliation on either him or themselves, and after much spiritual anguish had sent him to an Oppidan house instead.

But Bamber's charm, even on the Etonian scale, was such that he had been able to pass among the Oppidans. He was elected to Pop, the self-appointed school aristocracy, still I think at that time entitled to beat their juniors, and also to wear fancy waistcoats. I can't imagine Bamber beating anyone, but I can see him in a gold brocade waistcoat, and it suits him remarkably well. He cultivated Oppidan tastes and devoted his leisure time to shooting and fishing. He was proud to claim, he told me, that he had never read a single book that he hadn't been required to read, or written anything apart from a game diary, in which he recorded the totals of wildlife he had rid the world of.

This approach to life, which had served him so well at school, proved more problematic when he decided (somewhat oddly, given his views at the time) that he wanted to go on to Cambridge – and to read English literature. He had applied to King's, the intellectually distinguished college of Keynes and E. M. Forster, and a sister foundation of Eton, which made it the natural first port of call for high-flying Etonians. The interview with the senior tutor had not gone well. What were Bamber's leisure interests, he asked. Shooting and fishing, replied Bamber. The senior tutor, who had been spending his days listening to candidates boasting of their fascination with Sumerian pictographs and Riemannian geometry, had looked (so Bamber told me) a little surprised. 'Anything else?' he asked. Bamber said that he had been taken aback in his turn by the implication that shooting and fishing were not a perfectly adequate range of interests. But, quick as he always was, even in the philistinism he cultivated, he realised that the interviewer was perhaps hoping for evidence of something more cerebral. He had quickly searched his memory for the name of some learned pursuit that might qualify, and remembered seeing boys at school doing something that suggested seriousness . . . Of course! 'Reading, sir,' he said.

The senior tutor looked even more taken aback. So, reading. Quick though Bamber was, he had not foreseen the question that this would obviously lead to: what books had he been reading recently?

Which put him into even greater difficulties. The senior tutor waited. What bold claim was it going to be this time? Merely Gibbon and Proust again? Or something a little more adventurous? The *Epic of Gilgamesh*, perhaps, or the Rig Veda in Sanskrit? At last Bamber recalled a book that he had seen at any rate the outside of – a bestseller of the day that had been left lying about in his parents' otherwise book-free house by a visiting aunt, and one that had looked impressively bulky. '*The Cruel Sea*, sir,' he said. The senior tutor did his professional best to keep a straight face and continue the interview. 'What was it about?' he asked. 'The sea, sir,' said Bamber. And that was the end of his attempt to get into King's.

Back at Eton, and not before time, came the blinding flash from heaven. It was delivered by a fellow Colleger, Andrew Sinclair, an unashamed intellectual who had decided to make his career as a great writer. Andrew had read everything, certainly *Gilgamesh* and the Rig Veda, and probably written a few books already himself. By the end of the year, under Andrew's tutelage, Bamber, quick as ever, had become a fellow intellectual and read pretty much everything in his turn. Now fully armed he applied to Magdalene, traditional second port of call for Etonians who had failed to get into King's, where it turned out that all this new reading had been unnecessary after all. Bamber recalled only one question at his interview this time. 'Your uncle was at Magdalene, wasn't he? Yes . . . ? I think you'll be very happy here.'

All this I got from Bamber himself, recounted with his usual modesty and self-mockery, together with stories from his time as a national service subaltern in (of course) the Brigade of Guards, where he was (of course) a sought-after guest at the debutante balls of the London season. At Cambridge, even now he was an intellectual, he continued to be at home also in worlds of privilege still beyond the range of my explorations. So loved and admired was he that he survived even one of those make-or-break moments of truth that should have shut him out for ever. He was invited to join some truly appalling dining club whose members met to eat and drink – and drink – and drink – in eighteenth-century costume. The initiatory rite for new members was to stand and drink down a pint of claret. Bamber felt obliged to accept the challenge. He put on his cravat and knee-breeches and drank the claret. Before retiring first to vomit and then to resume his normal life, he cried with drunken passion, 'You're not my friends! William and Nicholas are my friends!'

I wish I could remember everything we said and did together for the rest of my last year. Only one magical evening comes to mind. I had been in Trinity, talking grandly about love and literature with Andrew Sinclair, Bamber's mentor, and missed the deadline by which visitors had to be out of college. I should have to climb out, and since it was a warm spring night, Andrew decided to come with me for an illicit midnight stroll on the moonlit Backs. The route out of Trinity was complex and mostly at rooftop level, with a long balancing act at one point along a high wall overlooking the Master's bathroom, where Lord Adrian, as I recall, was cleaning his teeth. The deserted silver lawns and dark elms around the river, when we reached them, were a landscape from a dream, and we decided we should like to share it with Bamber, whose rooms in Magdalene looked out over St John's Backs. So we threw gravel up at his window, like boys in a children's adventure story, until he woke up and shinned gracefully (of course) down the wall to join us. Then we walked around talking grandly about our differing literary techniques, self-consciously intoxicated by the moonlight and by being where we were not supposed to be and where no one else was. Also, I suppose, by having our lives and all their vast cloudy possibilities still unexplored in front of us.

A bit embarrassing to recall all this now. Were we trying to live out a kind of imitation *Brideshead*? Our little world of latter-day privilege wasn't really much like Waugh's lost paradise, though. Bamber himself was certainly no Sebastian Flyte. He had no taste at all for drunkenness or decadence, and he was far from indolent. He was as sober and ambitious as all the rest of us. He was just better at doing what all of us aspired to – looking as if we weren't.

He was certainly hard-working – but, he claimed, only in the mornings. He was reading English, and had reduced his list of books to the ones on which he had calculated there must necessarily be questions in Finals. The system was successful (of course) and he got a first, then went on to spend a year at Magdalene teaching, and another year in the US on one of those scholarships founded to promote mutual understanding between the privileged on either side of the Atlantic.

By this time I had already emerged into the so-called real world. Quite noticeably real, in my case – Manchester, all smog and wet red brick, and remarkably unlike Cambridge, though its gloom was slightly lightened by that weekly one-thirty-second of Bamber's royalties. So when he invited me to spend Christmas with him and his family in their country house in Scotland I was quick to accept. A little too quick, perhaps, because when I heard nothing more and doggedly phoned to check I realised he had forgotten all about it. I had to hold on while be belatedly told his parents that they had an uncovenanted extra guest.

So this was how I first met his family. Their country home in the holidays was the wing of a castle they rented on a shooting estate in Aberdeenshire. They had all the familiar, welcoming warmth, as if a socially dubious newspaper reporter with a weird haircut (I was trying something vaguely Roman at the time) was exactly the guest they had been hoping for to complete the family circle. Intimidating, nevertheless, to the reporter himself. Particularly Bamber's father, good casting for a choleric ex-colonel, now something grand in a City livery company, with a taste for shooting and vintage port, and a soft heart well hidden behind an alarmingly ferocious face and challenging abruptness of manner. One of his passions was gardening, and the gardens of the castle, under an arrangement with the National Trust of Scotland, were open to the public once a week. Members of the public who tried to get in on the wrong day, so Bamber told me, risked being chased back down the drive by Colonel Gascoigne with a horsewhip. His forebears were generals and landed gentry, and 'Bamber' was in fact a surname drawn from way back in the family annals. It had been bestowed upon its current and surely most illustrious bearer as a middle name, tucked modestly away behind an 'Arthur' which had somehow got lost along the way. Which was helpful for his later brand image. There have been many Arthurs in the world, but, so far as I know, only and unforgettably the one Bamber.

His mother had even grander origins. She was an O'Neill, from an Ulster dynasty which I think I recall Bamber as saying sprang in some complex way from the kings of Ireland. She had the same lively warmth and eager grace as Bamber himself, with perhaps a touch of Irish charm superadded, and was particularly assiduous in putting me at my ease; but then she would probably have done the same for even the Seven-headed Wild Beast of Revelation if one of her children had chosen to bring it home for Christmas. Then there was Bamber's younger sister Veronica, who was at Oxford and a noted beauty, with all the family grace; and Brian, still at Eton, who loved shooting and fishing, as Bamber had once done, but who also seemed able to play any musical instrument at sight, and who had mastered the bagpipes in time to pipe in the Christmas pudding.

The children treated their parents with perfect old-fashioned courtesy and respect, but were evidently able to stand their ground when they felt they had to. His father, Bamber explained to me, was a little disappointed in these apparently perfect children of his. In Bamber, for a start. His father had assumed that he would go into the City like himself, inherit the pipes of port he had laid down for him and eventually take over the running of the estate. It must have required unwonted forbearance to accept that Bamber was going to throw all this away by opting for Cambridge and a life in the media. It put the onus on Veronica to make a good marriage to someone with the virtues that Bamber lacked. This, it turned out, was not what she had in mind at all. In return for doing the London season, and hating every moment of it, she persuaded them to allow her to throw herself away in her turn by going to Oxford, after which she married William Plowden, who went on to become, not something in the City, but something in Whitehall – a high-flying and high-minded civil servant. She then led a life of public service and of ever more selfless devotion to others less fortunate than herself, which culminated in donating a kidney to a stranger. This left only Brian to rescue the family honour. It must have been the last straw when he turned out to be as brilliant as his brother and sister, took himself off to Cambridge in his turn, and then became a professional musician.

The family seemed able to negotiate all this wilfulness, however. There was certainly no hint of any conflict during that Christmas. Which was sumptuous. There were many guests besides me, either staying in the house or arriving by the Land Rover-load each morning, and all there for the shooting. I suspect that Bamber would have been obligingly going out with them each day himself, but realised that trying to include his dodgy friend from Cambridge would have been a step too far into social improbability, and instead lent me a .22 rifle and took me out to shoot a less ambitious target, pigeons. There was also skating on the frozen lake. Bamber, needless to say, was a swift and graceful skater – and turned out to be able to ride a penny-farthing without falling off. Then, when darkness ended the open-air day, a long, restoring soak in the bath, with bathrooms and hot water enough for everyone.

• • •

I realise that this must all sound a bit too good to be true, and I'm trying to think of a few faults in Bamber to lend the picture some plausible light and shade. Yes – occasional impatience; his quickness sometimes made it difficult for him to wait for those of us who moved more slowly in life. And his eagerness to make everyone happy sometimes led to difficulties in accommodating all the people he felt obligations to, or even remembering who they were. As, I think, in the case of his invitation for Christmas. And, yes – I know! A much worse failure: his total blindness to the interest of a subject that I had always found intensely engaging – philosophy.

This was the occasion for the only time I can remember seeing him lose his temper, and the only argument I ever had with him. Exactly what we had disagreed about always remained itself a matter of disagreement. I thought it was phenomenalism. I had been trying to explain, as I recalled it, why some philosophers (not me) had believed that physical objects were really the experiences we had of them. He believed that it was about Zeno's paradox of Achilles and the tortoise. Whichever it was, he found either the argument so silly, or the paradox so unparadoxical, that it enraged him, and he raised his voice and became quite uncharacteristically red in the face.

We were sitting in a restaurant in Italy at the time and we became aware that our fellow diners had all fallen silent and turned to look.

26

This was probably not because of any particular interest in phenomenalism or Zeno, we realised later, but because we were with Bamber's then girlfriend and they thought we were arguing over her.

Which in a way, perhaps, we were. Bamber and I had had a long-standing agreement to go to Italy together and I had spent the summer teaching myself basic Italian in preparation. At some point, though, he had fallen for another Cambridge star, a rather dazzling girl at Girton who had performed in both his triumphant revue and my untriumphant one, and, evidently forgetting about our arrangement, he had invited her to go to Italy with him. What would Bamber have done if our positions had been reversed? He would have stepped gracefully aside. I should have learned from his hypothetical example, as usual, and done likewise, but gracelessly did not. So he of course honoured both his obligations and tried to keep us both happy. Which he pretty much did. All the same, my presence must have been a bit of a damper, and my exposition of phenomenalism, or Zeno's paradox, was perhaps just too much for even Bamber to bear.

• • •

Perhaps, in the years that followed, as we both tried to establish ourselves in our careers, there was always just a hint of unacknowledged rivalry, as there probably is in most male friendships. I certainly felt a little outstripped when he later taught himself Italian in his turn – but did it in two weeks, and well enough to take up an invitation to give a lecture tour in Italy. He moved into my field, journalism, and began reviewing theatre for the *Observer*. Later we both published many books and at different times tried our luck with plays. But before that came the decisive breakthrough that set his course in life.

Granada Television had imported the formula for a new quiz show from America, to be called *University Challenge*, and was looking for potential quizmasters. I was doing a certain amount of television at the time and was one of the many people they invited to audition. I didn't wait to be rejected; I knew I should be out of my depth and was not surprised when they picked Bamber. He had every quality the job required: quickness and spontaneity, good humour and a sense of fun, an interest in everyone and everything. It even satisfied his intellectual ambitions and love of research, because he opted to compose his own questions.

He did it for the next twenty-five years, and was famous once again from the first moment onwards. But this time his success was nationwide. We walked up Helvellyn together one fine summer's day just after he had started doing the programme (his first experience of hill-walking, and I think his last, because he found it almost as irritatingly pointless as philosophy), and other walkers and climbers on remote parts of the mountainside waved and shouted, 'Hello, Bamber!' It was the same story wherever he went. I loved seeing him lit by the sunshine of celebrity, and feeling a little of it spilling over on to me by association. I was always delighted when I was occasionally mistaken for him by his admirers. And he had the grace to both take pleasure in his fame and remain completely unchanged by it.

• • •

The other event in those early years that defined the rest of Bamber's life was meeting Christina. I'm not sure when this was. I think when she was still at Girton, reading Persian. She was rather like Bamber – able, attractive and graceful. She had many admirers, and when she graduated and went off to travel as a photographer in Iran she was with one of them. I remember Bamber debating, with a seriousness and uncertainty I hadn't seen in him before, whether to take on the unaccustomed role of pursuer and go after her.

He went. And won her back. And for the next sixty years they were the perfect couple, travelling the world together to collaborate on books and becoming ever closer and more devoted to each other.

We were both absorbed in our own separate lives by this time, so I didn't see very much of them as they set up the home where they would spend the rest of their lives – another example of Bamber's talent for making stable and enduring arrangements. It was in Richmond, in a late-Georgian terrace overlooking the Thames, and together they turned it into the ideal setting for their lives. Bamber did a lot of the plumbing and electrics with his own hands. Christina painted the walls with arcadian murals and the floors with carpet patterns. They made two small but jewel-like gardens, back and front. In one of their two boathouses they housed the skiffs they rowed on the river, and the other they turned into Christina's workshop when she extended her range of professional activities from photography, painting and book illustration to pottery (all done with great distinction, particularly the pottery, with which she had a great and enduring success).

And of course one of the pleasures that Bamber took in this wonderful house was to give pleasure to others. By, among other things, inviting friends to swim in the river. Always, I think, early on summer Sunday mornings, and carefully timed to work with the rising and falling tides. Claire, my wife, felt as warmly about Bamber as I did, and it was getting to know Richmond through the swimming parties that made us first think of moving there. It's natural for friends to drift apart, as the circumstances of life that kept them together change with marriage, with new friends and new places to live. But now we became not only friends but neighbours again, separated by a comfortable mile's walk along the river and over the waterside meadows. It opened a kind of Indian summer in our relationship. By this time we were late in our lives and careers, and any possible shades of rivalry were long behind us. We had both in different ways had our successes.

And our disappointments. Mine were egregious – plays, mostly, very publicly garlanded with bad reviews and abrupt closures. Bamber had one theatrical flop of his own, but mostly it was difficult to know whether his hopes in life had been fulfilled or not because of his unshakeable cheerfulness and resilience. He published some twenty books, including short novels, history and travels. But nothing that he wrote ever quite replicated the irresistible charm of that show at Cambridge. His marriage seemed to be profoundly happy, but did he and Christina mind not having children? They would have been such wonderful parents. They didn't seem to mind – or even to notice. Why didn't I ever ask him, I wonder now. I don't really know. Why didn't he ask me why I *did* have children? Perhaps he wondered, but didn't ask because it would have seemed intrusive, and to have implied some possibility of criticism. And perhaps, in this as in so many things, I was consciously or unconsciously learning from his example. Perhaps simply because it seemed to both of us that what was, was.

The two great projects of Bamber's later years were massive off-shoots from *University Challenge*: *Encyclopaedia of Britain* and, even more ambitious, a digital encyclopaedia of world history that was based on his realisation of the possibilities that computers were opening up for people to make their own choices about how to select and use information – a digital databank of facts that could be arranged in any permutations you liked, to make 'timelines' of whatever historical narrative you were interested in following. He threw himself into the project with all the enthusiasm and energy of which he was capable. He raised the working capital, and he spent eleven years doing the research and inputting it into the system. It was a bold idea and he had hoped it would provide them with an income. But, although it's still much used, it was rather over-shadowed by the huge reach of Wikipedia and the universal search engines. And yet I never heard him utter a word of complaint, or saw a moment of depression.

As we became old men we both developed problems with our health. The most spectacular in his case were sudden losses of con-sciousness, caused possibly by low blood pressure, though doctors never seemed to be certain. Christina became very skilled at recog-nising the approach of one, such as starting to lean sideways as he walked. She would remain very calm and offhand, and force him to sit down before he fell. Sometimes he would become curiously unable to take any voluntary action to save himself, and she would kick him on the back of his knees so that his legs folded up and he collapsed into a waiting chair by gravity. He would apparently lose consciousness every morning when he got out of bed. Once he fell in the street and came down flat on his face on a hard pavement. Neighbours found him lying in a pool of blood, and for weeks his

face was masked by scar tissue. Once he passed out in the door-
way of the local cinema, once in a restaurant where the four of
us were having dinner. Christina, entirely calm, wanted simply to
leave him lying on the floor until he came round, but the people
at the next table had already rung for an ambulance. Perhaps they
told the controller who it was, because we ended up with not only
an ambulance but four other NHS vehicles lined up along the kerb
outside. In the teeth of Christina's objections he was removed to
the local A & E, where he was subjected to every known form of
heart and brain investigation. All negative, he told us cheerfully,
when we visited him in the hospital the following day. Then there
was a period when he couldn't walk more than a hundred yards.
Everything was fine, he told me. I didn't even know, until I made
a great fuss about having a pacemaker fitted, that he had had one
himself for five years without mentioning it.

• • •

It gave me pleasure to write this piece about him, and to remember
our sixty years of friendship. My pleasure was clouded, though, by
a growing unease about what he would feel himself when he read
it. He wouldn't have chosen, I knew, to have his virtues and the
warmth of my feelings about him so publicly proclaimed. But he
would reflect that if he objected it would spoil *my* pleasure – and
that if he asked me not to publish it the entire book would probably
be sunk. So he would feel obliged to conceal his disapproval, and I
should feel uneasier still.

By the time I sent him the finished text his health problems had come to a head, and he was taken into hospital, unable to walk or stand, to read or write, or even to think and speak coherently. At some point, though, in the midst of all this, he managed to read it and dictate to Christina a reassuring response for her to send me. He was far too delightfully flattered, he said, but was vastly enjoying it. I was very touched by this characteristically thoughtful effort to set my mind at rest, and even allowed myself to believe it a little. It wasn't true, of course. He *had* been embarrassed, Christina admitted to me. But, with no less characteristic thoughtfulness, she waited for a few days before she told me, until he was embarrassed no longer because he was dead.

• • •

A few years before all this, though, he had had an astonishing and entirely unforeseen reward for being who and what he was.

For years he and Christina had been selflessly visiting an elderly aunt of his, in spite of her being so senile that she couldn't remember who he was. What he didn't mention, when he sometimes told us stories of these confused encounters, was that she was a duchess – the Duchess of Roxburghe – and owned a vast country house in Surrey, West Horsley Place. Bamber knew that she had arranged to leave it to someone on the other side of her family, but when she died it turned out that, at some point when she still had a mind to change, she had changed it and left it to Bamber.

Overnight Bamber had become a country landowner, the proprietor of a fifteenth-century mansion with fifty rooms, vast gardens, outhouses, cottages and farms. Maybe inheritance, at any rate on this scale, is an injustice, and we should none of us inherit any-thing. But while the practice persists, this was surely the most just injustice ever. It was certainly one that gave Bamber not only sur-prise but great pleasure. A pleasure which he shared, so far as he could, like so many other pleasures, with his friends. He invited us all down to show us the gardens, the vast halls and staircases, the attics, the books and pictures, the late duchess's three diamond tiaras. He gave a New Year's Eve dinner in front of a blazing log fire in the great fireplace, at which we all almost died of hypothermia.

But, like all the other privileges bestowed on him from those grander worlds beyond our ken, it turned out that there was a price to be paid, not only in incipient frostbite, but in an incommen-surate amount of time, anxiety and labour. The house had been neglected for many years and was on the verge of collapse. Almost every one of its fifty rooms was blocked by fallen ceilings and ran-dom piles of rotting furniture. The beautiful red-brick Tudor facade was several inches out of true at the top; an inch or two more and the roof would fall in. Structural engineers were sent for, like con-sultants summoned to the sickbed of some moribund millionaire. Just to keep the house standing, they estimated, would cost some 5 million pounds.

Bamber got Sotheby's to organise a vast sale of the contents, which raised 8 million pounds. But there would also be inheritance tax to pay, and from a very compelling combination of necessity and altruism he gave his wonderful new house away to a charit-able trust, to become a local centre for study and crafts. Not that this absolved him from his burdens, because he felt himself morally obliged to serve on the board of the charity, and the anxieties that this generated darkened his remaining years.

There was one unequivocally wonderful result from his benefaction, though. By a remarkable stroke of luck Grange Park Opera were just then being eased out of their home at a country house in Hampshire, and the new trust took them in – with spectacular results. The founder and CEO of Grange Park, Wasfi Kani, happened to be a kind of human whirlwind, with an extraordinary ability to charm the wealth of the wealthy out of their pockets and turn it into music. In less than a year she and her associates had conjured up a full-scale working opera house in the overgrown woods behind the house, and were doing a first season that included *Tosca* and *Die Walküre*.

So now there's life in the old place again – more life, almost certainly, than it has seen in the previous five centuries, including a summer season of boiling human emotion and the music that expresses it, a tented city in the orchards like the Field of the Cloth of Gold, picnic hampers and champagne, dinner jackets and evening dress (some of them worn by us and Bamber's other fortunate friends).

And among us, of course, for those few last years, the moving spirit of this particular universe, as graceful and famous, as lucky and loved, as he had been after that earlier triumph in the theatre a half-century earlier.

Revenant

The past is a foreign country, said L. P. Hartley, and he might have added that writers of fiction pillage it as ruthlessly as traders have always pillaged other countries with no adequate means of defending themselves. Characters, landscapes, events – plundered wholesale, often with names and identifying marks falsified to conceal their origins. My depredations have usually been relatively circumspect. The odd gold coin or two filched from one site, a few shards from another; a mannerism remembered from someone I once knew, a few turns of phrase from someone else. Until, late in life, I went rather further.

I wrote a novel set in a little enclave of suburban streets very much like the ones I had grown up in. I based one of my central characters on myself as I remembered being around the age of ten or eleven, and another on my best friend at the time, David. He was a boy who had seemed to have every possible good fortune – an indulged only child with a playroom full of beautifully crafted model trains, elaborate construction toys and serious tools for wood- and metal-working, all tidily shelved and carefully maintained. He also had all the talents that I lacked and he played a very dominant role in my life. I struggled hopelessly to imitate his skill with his hands. He built an elegant puppet theatre and created lifelike actors to play in it; I built a ramshackle imitation with a severely disabled cast. He made an episcope, a pinhole camera, a crystal set, and all of them worked; I made an episcope, a pinhole camera, a crystal set, and none of them did. He also had an imagination – I had none. As we walked round the neighbourhood he recounted a long-running tale of a talking monkey and the island it ruled over; all I could invent was another monkey and another island. It was he who determined all the games we played and all the hobbies we took up. Under his command we hollowed out a camp in the middle of a local hedge, and from it conducted our own private war on Nazi Germany.

By the time we had grown up I had lost all contact with him, and I made my career by using the imagination that I had never had when I knew him, and inventing the fictions that I never could invent as well as he could. More than half a century went by, and as I struggled late in life to find a narrative focus for a novel I wanted to write about the way in which children (and adults) make sense of the world around them through the stories they tell themselves, he had come back into my head – and as much in command as ever. What I had remembered was something he had told me one day as we sat in his back garden drinking the lemon barley that his mother had just brought us for elevenses. 'My mother', he had said thoughtfully, as we watched her walk back to the house, 'is a German spy.'

I was astonished – even more astonished than I was by all his other initiatives. It had come out of nowhere, unsupported by any evidence, not suggested by anything that had happened – a pure spontaneous invention. It wouldn't have surprised me all that much to learn that his *father* was a Nazi agent – his father was horrible enough for anything. But his *mother*? Who was always so loving to him and so welcoming to me as his one friend? It was absolutely unbelievable!

40

But *had* I believed it, nevertheless? Well, yes, in the way that unbelievable things do get believed. It had taken on a kind of reality just by being said, as some of our latter-day politicians have discovered with their entirely unevidenced allegations of conspiracy and proclamations of unachievable futures. The reality was established because the words had been said by David, whose role it was to say things like this, and because it was obviously the start of another of our games. It was just too rich in enjoyable possibilities *not* to be true.

So what had happened? Had we actually played the game out? Had we put on false beards and shadowed his mother to her secret transmitter and her meetings with her German controllers? I couldn't remember. All I could remember was that simple dramatic headline to the story. Maybe we had kept her under surveillance for an hour or two, and then, when she failed to steal any secret plans or send any covert radio messages, had got bored and given up.

But now I began to wonder what would have happened if we had been a little more persistent in our efforts, and watched her not for an hour or two, but for a week or so. What, at the age of ten or eleven, would we have made of an adult life?

So the fictitious boy in the novel I was planning, whose name was Keith, made the same announcement about his own mother, as slavishly as I had adopted the idea of the talking monkey, and my narrative was under way. Very soon Keith and his friend Stephen were hidden in the camp they had set up, much like our own, but sited just opposite his house, and they were spying on all his mother's comings and goings. The events that followed I invented, but his mother remained very much as I remembered her – graceful, indulgent, amused at our antics. The father, too, was the father

41

I remembered – a cold-hearted and frightening tyrant who had cast the one dark shadow over my friend's good fortune in life. And the boys themselves were recognisable versions of my friend and myself. Keith at one point even held a carving knife to Stephen's throat, just as David had once held one of the chisels he kept so well sharpened to mine, a torture that I supposed Keith, and perhaps David, had learned from seeing his father exercise it on his mother. The country of the past seemed to me as open to exploitation as the fictitious one I was creating, and I felt free to import from it and adapt my imports exactly as I thought fit.

I had nearly finished the book when a very obvious and disconcerting thought came to me and stopped me short. The past, it suddenly struck me, was *not* a fiction. It had an objective reality that was shared with other people. Until that moment my friend had ceased to be quite real for me, in the sense of being a creature who could be affected by present events. He had been dematerialised by time, because for so long he had existed only in my memory. But if I was still alive, it belatedly occurred to me, then he might also be. In which case he would be a sentient creature just like me, with an awareness and feelings just like mine. He might read the book and recognise himself and his parents. He might not like what he read. He might be very hurt.

I tried to discover whether he was still alive, but I could find no trace of him. Eventually I put my scruples aside and went on with the book, but uneasily conscious that sooner or later I should have to decide whether to go ahead and actually release it to the world.

But the past, like any other foreign country, can spring surprises, and it was at precisely this point that it sprang one on me – one of the biggest surprises I have ever had.

It was a letter from David, my vanished friend. After more than half a century he had come looking for me, just as I had started looking for him.

'A voice from the past,' said the letter, and he reminded me that we had spent time together all those years ago, 'devising joint plans for fighting off the power of the Third Reich, sometimes from the centre of a farm hedge'. I might be surprised to hear that he was still alive, he said. He would love to hear from me if I was agreeable. And after his signature at the bottom, in case I still hadn't remembered who he was, he added: 'The one with the ferocious father.'

It was as if I had conjured him back from the land of shadows simply by thinking his name to myself. Or gone back to one of our favourite books, *101 Tricks a Boy Can Do*, and at last managed to do the hardest of them – making someone appear out of nowhere.

I realised, as I gradually recovered from my astonishment, that there was an explanation for the coincidence. As he said in his letter, 'There comes a time in life when the past starts to occupy a proportion of one's thoughts. I think they call it old age.'

So of course I had to write back and agree to meet him. And I had to confess what I was doing. I was writing a novel, I told him, about two fictitious characters who had 'certain resemblances' to the two of us, one of them with a sympathetic mother and a frightening father. He invited me to come and see him, and he turned out to be not a ghost from beyond the Lethe but a normal human being, now getting on in years, much like myself, and living in a converted oast house in the middle of the Sussex countryside with his second wife. He had two grown-up sons and had made a career as a photographer. This was the least surprising thing about him, because he had taken up photography when I had known him as a boy and become extremely skilled at it. I shouldn't have predicted, though, the sort that he specialised in – what is apparently known in the trade as glamour photography. He had made a studio in his barn, and he invited a regular stream of young models down from London, posed them artistically and lit them romantically, naked, under the distant but reassuring chaperonage of his wife. In fact he had become an acknowledged expert in the field and had written textbooks on it.

He had tried other lines of work, he said, most of them depending on the skill he had always had with his hands. He made bespoke cameras for professional photographers – beautiful creations of teak and brass, as they seemed to me, that could be configured to photograph high buildings without distortion, or revolve panoramically on clockwork turntables to take in long rows of schoolchildren. But no one, he said, had wanted to buy them. He had turned to handmade furniture and had built at any rate one piece, a massive and beautifully crafted dresser, as I could see for myself because he couldn't find a customer for it, and it was standing in his own living room. Nothing had worked, he said, and he had gone back to the naked models. He didn't much like them as people, or the time he spent working with them. Everything in his life had been a failure.

He had followed my career with interest, he said, and in comparison with his own it must have seemed one that I could be relatively content with. I found the painful discrepancy in our fortunes, and the reversal of our standing with each other, embarrassing. It got worse. He had decided to try an entirely new venture, one that had nothing to do with his undoubted and long-established technical and handicraft skills. He was moving into my field – he had written a book.

This is something that professional writers are not entirely

pleased to hear, possibly from fear of competition, but more probably – particularly when the new author confesses, as David did,
that he has already sent the manuscript to a long list of agents and
publishers without success – because they know that they will be
expected to offer to read it, and that the hope hangs in the air, even
if it remains unexpressed, that we will then recommend it to our
contacts in the business and get it published. Something about my
reaction, he said in his next letter, made him suspect that this was
what I was thinking – 'or perhaps worse it was the dark motive I
had in contacting you in the first place'. He assured me that this
was not what he had intended, and I think, on reflection, that my
suspicions were unworthy. He simply wanted to talk about the past,
just as I wanted to write about it.

But of course I still had to make the offer. Which meant that I
found myself reading his book before I had even finished mine, and,
tactful as I was about it, I became even more apprehensive about
how he would react to mine in his turn. When I had at last finished
it, though, and nerved myself to send it to him, he responded with
a generosity that I found rather astonishing. He had been greatly
entertained by it, he said, and it had brought those wartime summer days instantly back to mind. 'Obviously I read avidly about the
dreadful Keith. He is even worse than I feared . . . I expect the truth
of it was even more ghastly than the fiction.' He enclosed a detail
from a photograph of us both when we were still at the same local
school. He is seated – tidy, self-contained, his sharp features composed and watchful, like some small alert creature of the hedgerows.
I am standing behind him, like a manservant behind his master, my
short-sighted eyes screwed up uncertainly.

I was very relieved that he was prepared to accept my fictitious

versions of us both. I was even more relieved that he was happy
with the depiction of Keith's mother. He was sure, he said, that his
mother would have been highly diverted to find herself suspected of
being a German spy and also having a relationship with a character
who had a little in common with one of my uncles.

What he had liked most, though, was the cold, cruel tyrant I had
based on his father.

> He was all the things you say he was. Do you know he used
> to stand at the train window on his way home, as it passed
> our garden, to check that I was not doing anything dire to the
> lawn . . . His problem in reality was with the word 'play' . . . He
> believed in the work ethic. If work was to be effective it had, like
> medicine, to be as horrible as possible to be any good. Play was
> fun so it could not be countenanced at all. As you were always
> asking me to come out and 'play', you can see the problem.
>
> In fact the only reason that I took up photography is that it
> provided an escape from what he wanted me to do: working in
> a bank or an insurance company. That was work and what I did
> was not a proper job. He came to pretend I didn't exist. Even so
> he dominated my life and I feared him to his dying day. By then
> it was too late for me to get myself together and make any sense
> of what I was doing.

I was relieved that he felt I had not been unjust to his father's
memory. But I was appalled to discover the extent of the devas-
tation that his father had wreaked upon him – to see how he had
turned my friend's advantages in life to dust, devalued his skills
and imagination, undermined his self-confidence and poisoned his
pleasure in the world, and had gone on long after he had died,
still operating from beyond the borders of the past. I suppose that,

when David had identified his kind-hearted mother as the agent of an evil power, he had been transferring his feelings about his all-powerful father to a less terrifying object, rather as the religious blame anyone but their all-powerful god for the world's evils.

Another nineteen years went by after our strange reunion, and his luck didn't change. Christmas was coming round again, and I sent him and his wife Prue one of the comic Christmas cards I had made, decorated with a photograph I had taken using perhaps my pale imitation of his skills (though without the naked models). A card in return arrived from his wife. 'I am very sad to have to tell you', said the message inside briefly, 'that David passed away suddenly on Sunday. He collapsed whilst in his workshop.'

So the story had been brought to a close, and yes, it was another surprise, and a saddening one. But eighty-eight is a fair age, and death had come suddenly, while he was busy in the workshop where he done so many good things in the course of his life. As I told his widow in my letter of condolence, one would have to say that it was a good end at the last.

I had been planning for some time to write down my memories of him and the story of his surprising reappearance in my life. So I did, and here it is. I finished by sending my greetings across the frontier into the land of shadows after him, together with my thanks for all the games we once played and all the skills I at any rate half-learned from him, for the story that I had made from it all, and for the tolerance and understanding with which he had accepted it.

There turned out to be one or two more surprises still to come, though.

The first was as I finished these notes, when I wanted to check what I remembered saying in my letter of condolence. I looked in the file on my computer where I keep the copies of outgoing letters, but it wasn't there. I searched all the places where I might just imaginably have misfiled it. It was in none of them. It was as if I had never written it.

Odd, certainly. But perhaps I never *had* written it, I decided finally. What I remembered so clearly was not actually writing but intending to.

This was embarrassing, because a month or so had gone by since Prue had told me the news. I wrote another letter – did actually write it this time, and send it, with awkward apologies for not having done it sooner. Slightly odder still, though: she wrote back to tell me that I'd said it all already – that I *had* written before.

This was even more embarrassing. But if I hadn't written the second letter she wouldn't have written again in her turn, and I should probably never have found out what she now went on to say:

I didn't tell you the whole story about David's death. He did, in fact, take his own life.

It was Sunday afternoon 6th December and David was suffering from a nosebleed which he had from time to time but this particular one wouldn't stop, even though we tried everything. It eased off so I went to wash my hair and when I came down he wasn't there. I looked all over the house, in the garden and with my neighbour's help, even in the field behind the house. I eventually called the police who arrived with dogs to search surrounding areas. One policewoman eventually shone her torch into the workshop and saw a body on the floor. Russell, David's son, broke the door down which was locked on the inside, and saw his father there, having cut his wrists.

So I was wrong; it hadn't been such a good end. It seemed to be made somehow even more distressing by the odd domestic circumstantiality of the events – the nosebleed and the hair-wash. I thought about that ordinary Sunday afternoon in the winter countryside, with Christmas coming, and another of his tediously familiar nosebleeds happening. Then his retiring to the workshop where he was probably most at home, perhaps with some specific job he had in mind to do. Then looking at the blood on his handkerchief, and this recurring minor annoyance suddenly seeming just one misfortune too many to endure. Perhaps it was the sight of the spilt blood that put the idea into his head for how to deal with it, and all the other disappointments before it. So he carefully locked the door and went to the rack of meticulously sharpened tools over his workbench . . . And for a moment I felt again the edge of the one he had held against my own skin a lifetime earlier.

His widow said in her letter she thought he had been planning to end his life. She mentioned his low self-esteem and suggested its source. 'As you said, his father was not a nice person, and there is no question that he damaged David, and hence his lack of self-confidence.' I remembered David's telling me how he had feared him 'to his dying day'. And beyond, it seemed to me, to his own dying day.

That unfathomable country of the past! Once again a hand had reached out from its shadows. And taken a victim, chosen at its own good pleasure, back across the frontier with it.

Know-all

Of all the clever people I have been fortunate enough to meet during my life I think the cleverest was probably Eric Korn. Not the most intelligent, perhaps, but the cleverest, yes.

I first became aware of him on the top deck of a bus in Cambridge. It was conveying a batch of us, national servicemen who were being trained as Russian interpreters, back from the Slavonic Department in Station Avenue to our billets. It would have been difficult not to notice him, because he was parading about the central aisle loudly showing off his cleverness to the people sitting around him. I recall him as wearing an RAF uniform of egregious scruffiness, but, since the Department had refused to teach us in uniform, it was probably the demob suit that he had been issued with as a replacement, so scruffy in its turn that it was difficult to distinguish as such. He was short and dark, with thick spectacles and thick eyebrows; a kind of young Groucho Marx. A shameless cleverstick, and I remember how irritating I found the sight and sound of him on that bus – the bumptiousness, certainly, but also in some obscure way the scruffiness, the short-ness, the thickness of his glasses and eyebrows. What I can't now remember is how we got from this unpromising start to becoming friends – in fact, to his taking my defective education in hand and introducing me to science and modern literature, and some of all the thousand other things he was so clever about.

He had been at St Paul's School, I discovered later, with Oliver

Sacks, the neurologist who became famous with *The Man Who Mistook His Wife for a Hat*, and Jonathan Miller, much celebrated as a polymath – though not even Jonathan knew as much as Eric. Like them, he had been inspired to a passion for science by a legendary teacher at St Paul's, Sid Pask. But his intellectual ambitions had begun long before that. At the age of twelve (so he told me) he had decided to master the whole of human knowledge. He proposed to do this by reading every single volume in the EUP Teach Yourself series. I think there were then about seven hundred of them, ranging from *Teach Yourself Dressmaking* to *Teach Yourself Zulu*, and he had got halfway through before he realised that even all seven hundred of them might still not completely cover the world's stock of possible knowledge. So he abandoned them and turned to his own resources. By the time I got to know him, some seven or eight years later, he had pretty much reached his goal unaided. Or so it seemed to me, as I caught some of the bountiful overspill. A considerable part of what little I now know I first learned from Eric.

Or Erik, with a 'k', as he then was, at an intermediate stage between being Michael, as he had started out in life, and Eric with a 'c', as he became later. Why 'Erik' I don't think he ever explained, but his renaming himself, like his plans for omniscience, was one aspect of his taste for romantic self-invention. One of the models he had based himself on was a literary hero – Doc, in John Steinbeck's *Cannery Row*, who was also 'deceptively small', also clever and ambitious to know everything. Doc was a marine biologist, and it may have been Doc as much as Sid Pask who suggested the same career path to Erik. He was already embarking upon it when we first met, so it was handy when we were moved from Cambridge to a continuation course in Cornwall, within reach of the sea and of the Marine Biological Association's Laboratory in Plymouth. One of the people on our course had a car, and we used to cadge rides from him at the weekend. Then I would spend the Sunday morning idling on the beach while Erik collected specimens, and the afternoon in the Association's laboratory on the seafront, reading the reviews in the *Observer* while he dissected what he'd found, and followed it through the microscope into a magic world of his own.

He also wrote poetry and revue sketches, both better than the various aspiring writers and entertainers on the course did. We became joint editors of *Samovar*, or *Самовар*, our bilingual literary magazine. His Russian was good, and the best thing we ever published in the magazine was his vividly eloquent translation of the great (and difficult) valedictory poem that Mayakovsky wrote before his suicide. I'm not sure quite how many other languages he could read, but he once complained to me, when I went on later to read Modern Languages at university, that this required an acquaintance with only two of them, whereas he and his fellow scientists were expected to master, on top of their full-time science studies, half a dozen well enough to read and deliver papers in them.

He introduced me to cybernetics (the forerunner of computer science), comparative philology, John Dos Passos and Budd Schulberg, and I think to Ronsard and Rabelais. In the southwestern suburbs of London, where I grew up, I'd scarcely met a Jew, and it was Erik who first introduced me to Jewish customs and practices. He had no religious belief himself, but he showed me the austere beauty of Bevis Marks, the Orthodox synagogue in the City, and made me see why Jews, as a small minority in the population, would want to preserve their identity and their traditions. He was also impartially interested in Christian mysticism; he made me read the *Four Quartets* and explained about St John of the Cross and the dark night of the soul. In Cornwall we spent a lot of time hunting for the Holy Grail. He had been persuaded by Flavia Anderson's *The Ancient Secret* (and had persuaded me in my turn) that it was not a Christian but a pre-Christian cult object – a lens or mirror used by the Druids to exercise their prerogative of creating fire, and associated with King Arthur – and our search charged the whole West Country with magical significance. Years later, when I wrote the first edition of my new column in the *Guardian* and realised it coincided with Rosh Hashanah, the Jewish New Year, he supplied all the information and contacts I needed to take it as my opening subject.

What did I do for him in return? Nothing, really. There was nothing I knew that he didn't – except how to drive. So I taught him to drive, as I had a number of friends. Or rather totally failed to. Orchestrating clutch, brake, gear, traffic signals and the behaviour of other motorists he plainly found harder than anything in calculus or particle physics. We had at last come up against a limit to his infinity, as unexpectedly as explorers falling off the edge of the world.

National service ended and we all resumed the interrupted trajectories of our lives. A dozen of us had places waiting at Cambridge – and now, of course, friends to see us through those first terms that many students find so bleak. Another dozen of us, Erik among them, were going to Oxford, which gave both groups a destination for mutual weekend visits. Also, I need hardly say, the occasion to found a new inter-university literary magazine to accommodate the rich surplus of our talents, printed in italic, on grey paper. I was the Cambridge end of the enterprise, but the only contributions of any interest originated in Oxford – a piece of poetic prose by Alan Bennett and a couple of whimsical items by Oliver Sacks, all I assume secured by Erik, together with a poem by a genuinely accredited poet, Dannie Abse, that was by some odd circumstance actually readable, which almost justified the whole sloping grey enterprise. The magazine was called *Seed*, which sounds the kind of earnestly dull title that literary magazines are given, but which for us had another reference altogether. A Seed, in our private vocabulary, was not a little organism you planted in the ground but a human being – someone who embodied the noble seediness of dress, manners and thought that we had learned to affect during our national service in resistance to the nation's attempts to smarten us up; one of us, in other words. What *Les Temps modernes* was to existentialism, *Seed* was to be to seediness. It lasted one issue.

Erik was reading either biology or zoology, I can't remember which, and his tutor was the great Dutch biologist Nikolaas Tinbergen. Tutorials often consisted of watching Tinbergen's famous sticklebacks while Tinbergen himself seized the chance to slip out at last for something to eat. Still only a first-year undergraduate, and he was already doing cutting-edge research with a world-famous scientist! He was at Queen's, and he had a magnificently sited room over Culpeper's the herbalist's, on the corner of the High and Queen's Lane. It was here, on one of the Cambridge contingent's weekend visits to Oxford, that he introduced me to yet another amazing new world – Wittgenstein and the *Tractatus Logico-Philosophicus*. It was the first time I had heard of either, and I think the discovery may have been one of the things that first got me interested in a philosopher – and a subject – that were going to have an enduring influence on my life. '*Die Welt ist alles, was der Fall ist,*' it began bilingually, on facing pages, which gave it a wonderful inherent importance – 'The world is everything that is the case.' And at once I see again the wooden pestle and mortar that sat on the ledge just outside Erik's window – Culpeper's sign, but to me the emblem that informed the world of Erik's place of residence and seat of learning.

During the working week the conversation would continue by postcard and letter. I have a file full of the correspondence from his side, but it's difficult now to make sense of because it's mostly undated, and, even when it's typed, done with such heroic seediness, and so nobly devoid of paragraph breaks and other conveniences traditionally resorted to by Thicks and Solids (the two categories to which Seeds assigned the rest of the human race). In one letter he complains that my last to him had been so unseedily well typed that it had taken him only a minute to read. In the undergrowth of his letters there are invented quotations from Norse sagas, and many snatches of Dutch, a favourite language. He even tried to keep Royal Mail entertained. The envelope of one letter is addressed:

Postman, let me please explain,
Deliver this to   M J FRAYN
Residing at   EMMANUEL COLLEGE
(chaste, in the pursuit of knowledge)
– he learns to tell the True from shams
Where else, but at   CAMBRIDGE,
                                         CAMBS

When I spent the Christmas vacation one year working in a refugee camp with Hungarians who had fled after the 1956 rising, he came down with two friends, Veronica and Dick, to cheer my exile, and telegraphed to warn me in a language as irresistible as Dutch – the telegraphese that newspapers then famously used in order to save money in their cables to and from correspondents by keeping down the number of words. They planned to arrive during the early afternoon in a week's time, he explained. Or rather:

VERONDICCUM DETRAINING WEEKWISE PROTOPOSTMERIDIALLY
— ERIK

Back in London during the vacations we walked round the West End together, he mostly talking, me mostly listening. We spent hours reading our way through the more obscure bookshops in Charing Cross Road, or Bernard Kops's famous book barrow just off Cambridge Circus, or Luzac's the orientalist's in Great Russell Street. There were relatively few Indian or Asian restaurants in London then, and he was at home in at any rate all the cheaper ones. He dared himself on to hotter and hotter vindaloos. Once, in a greasy spoon where there was nothing more interesting on the menu than a mixed grill, he cheered it up a bit by eating the management's tulips as a side-dish.

Out on the streets again he would break off his learned commentary every now and then to point out some landmark we were passing – the house where God lives (the Athenaeum), or an employment agency for waiters and prostitutes (the French primary school in Noel Street, with its traditional separate entrances for *garçons* and *filles*). We often made a detour on our peregrinations to pass through Fortnum and Mason. Not that we could afford to buy anything, but one of the tailcoated floorwalkers there seemed to recognise him, and always bowed to him. Perhaps he was simply impressed by Erik's pre-eminence in the seediness we aspired to. Cords and a British warm, of course – a duffel coat – which most students at the time wore, but somehow even more remote than anybody else's from any possible suspicion of elegance, and set off by an elderly and exhausted clip-on bow-tie (probably inspired by Steinbeck's Doc), which was not quite so firmly attached to him as he was to it. In some Malayan or Philippine restaurant one night, while he was explaining Mazdaism to me, or Gertrude Stein, or wave–particle duality, or trying (successfully, I have to report) to persuade me that truffles were the faeces of peach-fed pigs, the aged tie lost its last faltering grip on life and fell into his soup. Without pausing or even glancing down he fished it out, shook off the soup, and clipped it back on his collar.

His father was a trader in a traditionally Jewish line of business – precious metals – and his speciality was calling on the dentists of North London to buy the scraps of amalgam that collected in the traps beneath the basins their patients rinsed into, and recovering the mercury and silver from them. His success in the trade had enabled Michael (as his parents still thought of Erik) to escape by way of St Paul's School into the completely different world where I met him. It was still intensely Jewish. He would invite me to join him and his friends, all old Paulines and all Jews, on a Saturday evening after the end of the sabbath, perhaps in the Cosmo, the traditional German Jewish coffeehouse at Swiss Cottage, or being driven around North-West London by Oliver Sacks, who had access to a car, with everyone talking at once – everyone except the only Gentile, overawed by their brilliance and cohesiveness as a group, and feeling the same slight bracing tingle of self-consciousness that lone Jews must so often have felt in Gentile society.

In the Easter vacation of 1955 Erik made a sudden dramatic move from talk to action. On 5 April Winston Churchill, the prime minister, resigned. It was one of the biggest stories of the year – but the engineers and electricians on the London evening newspapers were on strike, so there were no print media to report it. Erik decided that he and I should seize the opportunity and produce an evening paper of our own to fill the gap. Our third joint essay into journalism, this time devoted not to a few sensitive literary maunderings that no one wanted to read, but to an unrepeatable exclusive on a major national news story. Not for a tiny readership of disaffected students, but a potential metropolitan audience of 12 million.

I can't remember now whether our aim was to provide a public service or to launch careers as press barons. I'm not sure we stopped to think, any more than we really had with *Samovar* or *Seed*. The point was to act – now, today, as soon as I could get into town, so that we could have it on the streets in time to catch the commuters on their way home. We needed a printing plant, of course, but at such short notice had to settle for a copying machine – the only one we could find, which was in Jonathan Miller's house. We'd got the story and the rest of the day's news – I suppose from the radio – written them up, laid them out, and were well into the print run for the first edition when a problem arose – an unsettling suggestion from Jonathan that what we were doing amounted to strike-breaking. We hadn't thought of it like that, and it slowed us down a bit. Then another problem stopped us completely. Jonathan's father was a distinguished psychoanalyst, and the copying machine – *his* copying machine – was just out-side his consulting room. As each copy emerged the machine signalled its achievement, like a hen squawking to announce she's laid an egg, by ringing a bell, and, after three or four hours of enduring this musical accompaniment to his patients' dreams and childhood memories, he called a halt.

By this time we had I suppose two or three hundred copies ready for distribution. Distribution, yes . . . this was a side of the news-paper industry that we hadn't yet had time to think about. I don't recall being involved in this phase of the operation. I suppose I'd gone home to the suburbs exhausted, and I was relieved to get a phone call from Erik later that evening to say that he had disposed of the entire print run – a much better result than we had achieved with *Samovar* or *Seed*. He had met a man outside Marble Arch Tube station, he told me, who had kindly agreed to take the whole stock off his hands and to meet us in the Cosmo the following morning with the proceeds. Next day the two of us sat over our cappuccinos in the Cosmo waiting for him. We sat there for a long time. We couldn't phone our distributor to find out where he was because Erik hadn't thought to ask him for his phone number. Or even his name.

At some point in that year he launched into an even more improbable enterprise than press proprietorship. He got engaged. This was surprising enough. In his first year at university? When his attention was so taken up by *Seed* and his tutor's sticklebacks? Even more surprising was his choice of fiancée – Marianne Macdonald, Molly, a Canadian graduate student who was writing a thesis on Ezra Pound. I'd met her with him on my weekends in Oxford. She seemed more like an aunt than a girlfriend, and she treated him with a patronising sarcastic humorousness, as if he were a rather comically slow-witted child.

When I showed this piece to Eric's widow from his second marriage, Olga Shaumyan, she told me something more surprising still. There had already been someone else in his life, whom I had never heard him so much as mention – Maggie Angus, an artist some five years older than him who lived in Cambridge. How on earth had he managed to have any kind of relationship with someone in Cambridge? When we had been there on the Russian course we had all been leading lives entirely cut off from anyone outside the Slavonic Department. Then at Oxford those first terms had surely been fully taken up with sticklebacks and italic prose, and his occasional weekends in Cambridge had been spent with his old friends from the Russian course. But this was only the beginning of my astonishment. For the sake of this Maggie Angus, whose existence he never mentioned, and whom he can have known scarcely better than the man outside Marble Arch Underground station, he had apparently considered converting to Catholicism. Catholicism?! Erik? The extraordinary things one can sometimes find out, sixty or so years after the event, about people one thought one knew! After this brief excursion out of *Cannery Row* into *Brideshead Revisited* his engagement to Molly seems rather less bizarre.

But *were* they in fact engaged? I can't remember now how I had heard, but I evidently passed the news on to a mutual acquaintance at Cambridge, because a remarkably forceful denial from Erik arrived in my pigeonhole at college. 'Dear Mike,' it said (and he is almost the only person who has ever called me that; perhaps he resisted my 'Michael' as much as he did his own).

Dear Mike

    You bastard. You shit.

    I hate your guts.

    As a confidant you rate pretty low.

    As a gossip you're pretty bloody inaccurate.

    PBN [the mutual acquaintance] says Molly and I are engaged.

    We're not.

    Mind your own fucking business.

    If we were it would be private.

    You would have been told.

    The entire student body of Cambridge would not have been.

    Kindly publish denials at your own expense. ERIK.

I presumably withdrew and apologised, and by the time he wrote again he was his usual good-humoured self. Though whether that self was engaged or not remained unclear:

> Take it easy don't get me wrong . . . The point being that though we both think it an excellent idea, no announcements have been made and we have agreed not to make up our own minds for certain – though what that means I don't know. In view of opposition from both our families – but mainly mine, who happen to be nearest, premature announcements would be peculiarly damaging. Hence my rage, now appeased.
>
> I haven't thought of a suitable rumour for you . . . I may have told Derek Whitelock that you were reading for Orders.

At some later point the ambiguity seemed to be resolved; Erik had decided they were *not* engaged. It was Molly who told me, and she was so distressed that I took it upon myself to reproach him. Had he backed away, I asked him sententiously, simply because she wasn't Jewish? I was surely being even more meddlesome than I

64

had been before, but he responded this time with patience, and an implication that I had perhaps been right:

> Thank you for writing. I know you're trying to help, but surely it must have struck you that the points you make have all been my constant thinking companions for the last few weeks. I've been doing some steady introspection and I know it isn't conscious Jewish solidarity – otherwise I would have said. How far unconscious pressures have acted on me is one for the long winter evenings.

So it was definitely off. Except that they then proceeded to get married. Exactly when, I have no recollection – some time during that same busy first year at university, I think – nor where or how, which suggests that it must have come as rather a surprise to all of us. In spite of the opposition they had encountered from both their families, and her curiously condescending way of relating to him, they remained together for a dozen years or so and had two children. In the later years of their marriage she gave up English studies and took to breeding large dogs. They moved to a house in a commercial backstreet in Camden, which seemed, when my wife and I called one day while Molly and the dogs were away, to be furnished with very little except thousands of books and tens of thousands of visibly hopping dog fleas, for which our feet and lower legs served as emergency food aid.

It was while they were still living in Oxford that Erik and I made yet another attempt to collaborate on a journalistic enterprise. I was already working as a reporter on the *Guardian* by this time, and was in Oxford one night (sleeping, I think, on the Korns' floor – another good turn I probably never repaid) to cover several stories, and also, simultaneously, in the *Guardian* style, to review a touring theatrical production at the Playhouse. I persuaded the paper to let me offload at any rate the review on to a brilliant local writer I knew. Erik lived up to all the expectations I had aroused and wrote a very funny piece mocking the performance given by the star of the show, Elizabeth Seal. It was only the following morning, when he bought the *Guardian* and read his copy in print, that it occurred to him there was something odd about the name, and he realised that when he had said 'Elizabeth Seal' it wasn't Elizabeth Seal he had meant, it was another actress completely, Elizabeth Sellars. Neither Miss Seal nor Miss Sellars, it turned out in the course of the next few days, was happy with the transposition. Nor was the *Guardian*, and Erik's career as a theatre critic went the same way as his career as a press baron.

So, back to biology, and the research he had started to do, which involved dissecting snails. There was a lot to be said for snails as a subject; at least they didn't steal your work, or threaten legal action if you got their identities mixed up. On the other hand they were small, and their insides were slippery. Erik – or had he settled into being Eric by this time? – told me that he had found experimenting on them even further outside his practical abilities than driving a car had been. Snail after snail, he said, had slipped away from his fumbling fingers, or got itself sliced up in unexpected ways. He began the work at Southampton University, and moved on, perhaps because the supply of snails in the south of England was running low, to McGill, in Toronto. Then, possibly because Ontario was getting short of snails in its turn, back to England and a new start at Liverpool, where he gave up the dissecting knife. He had discovered that LSD, then much in vogue for its psychedelic effects, also had an interesting effect, I think physical rather than mental, on snails. It seemed kinder to the snails – and it took a lot less dexterity. He laid in a large supply – and it was all stolen by his students. An inquiry followed, and the end of his career at Liverpool. Or anywhere else in academe.

And now, after so many false starts, he at last found his true path in life. I don't know quite how it happened, because we had rather lost touch with each other by this time, but he took up book-dealing, with a specialised interest in old scientific books. The vast range of his reading and scientific interests turned out to have a practical application, and he seemed to have developed the head for business that had been so notably lacking in his dealings outside Marble Arch Tube station. He began to travel the world's book fairs, became a successful and well-known figure in the business, and even more famous as a columnist in first the *Guardian*, then the *Times Literary Supplement*.

So a happy ending – two parallel happy endings. Three, in fact, because he got married again, to Olga Shaumyan, a Russian linguistician at Sussex. No – four, because by this time I had at last had a chance to make some small recompense for all the benefits he had conferred on me. The BBC asked me if I would be interested in taking part in *Round Britain Quiz*. Flattered as I was, I had enough sense to realise that I couldn't do it. I didn't know anything, and even what little I did know took me an unworkably long time to retrieve from my memory and put into words. There was one thing I did know, though, and could tell them at once, and that was the name of the person they really needed. This time it worked out, and for I think about a decade Eric and his teammate Irene Thomas represented London in the programme with such success that they apparently sometimes had to be handicapped.

Four happy endings – until they were all overtaken and eclipsed by another ending altogether. My last sight of him was at his eightieth birthday party, in a care home somewhere off the North Circular Road. He was sitting at the tea table in the day room, surrounded by friends and relatives, staff and fellow patients, with all kinds of good things to eat that Olga had brought, evidently still loved by everyone, smiling softly, but saying not a word – his mind swept as clean by dementia as one of those long-lost Cornish beaches by the falling tide. From all that teeming main of knowledge, all that quickness, all that invention, all that fun, all that fame, all that sheer cleverness – not a trace was left. Nothing except a few stranded specimens like these, collected and preserved in the memories of his surviving friends.

Balloon from Saratov

'*Gospoda!*' she would always begin when she addressed us – 'Gentlemen!'

A striking start. This was at the Joint Services School for Linguists, in the early fifties, in its rambling warren of knocked-together houses and temporary shedding in Station Avenue, Cambridge. We were all national servicemen. In the preceding months, on the barrack squares of various bleak army and air-force units, we had got used to being called by a great variety of names. 'Gentlemen' was not among them.

Dame Elizabeth Hill was Professor of Slavonic Studies and director of the School. Yelizavyeta Fyodorovna, as she was to her Russian colleagues, or Lisa, as all the rest of us called her, with a mixture of affection and awe. Born in St Petersburg in 1900, and totally bilingual, with a disconcerting compulsion, developed I suppose originally as a pedagogic aid, to repeat in the other language whatever she had said in either.

So, into the classroom she would sweep, the professor herself, her hair brushed flat around her broad brow and back into a matronly bun like an old-fashioned doll's, always smiling, with eyes of child-like innocence and inquisitorial penetration, as unpredicted and unpredictable as the inspector general, often in the middle of a class someone else was conducting, on a sudden fancy to take it herself instead. And – '*Gospoda!*'

She invested the word with such energy and forcefulness, such urgency and sincerity, that for a moment we almost believed that we *were* something faintly like gentlemen, perhaps even fellow scholars and Slavists. Then the fusillade would begin. Impossible texts for oral translation plucked without warning out of the air, terrible permutations of the different possibilities offered by the Russian verbs of motion, perhaps – going on foot/by some means of transport, perfective/imperfective aspect, determinate, indeterminate or frequentative – in all their various nightmare irregularities. 'The man who . . . often used to drop in at the house (on foot),' she would begin, 'having noticed two geese sliding along the street in a sledge, will tomorrow go several times, either on foot or in an electric tram . . .' Pause, while she struggled to imagine how to bring this farrago to a conclusion, and everyone else in the room waited to see who the finger was going to be pointing at. Then, offhand, thrown away with an impatient wave of the hand: '. . . to see his elderly aunt arrive by balloon from Saratov.'

And the finger would be pointing at *you*, and she would be nodding with eager encouragement, smiling with delight at the effortless correctness with which you were going to negotiate all those terrible verbs, coaxing the Russian out of you by the sheer brightness of her eyes. As inconspicuously as possible, the first verb would creep out of your mouth . . . the wrong one, naturally, representing the sort of dropping-in done not by an assiduous pedestrian but by the most infrequent horseman. Instant impatience from Lisa. You would be brushed aside, together with all your stupidity, in one characteristically Russian sweep of the hand in front of the face, and the bright expectant eyes would be shining on someone else. We could all do imitations of her, and often did, sometimes to her face.

I've always thought of her as the personification of everything most indomitable and transcendent in the Russian character, a wilful nineteenth-century landowner like Chekhov's Anna Petrovna, perhaps, or an eighteenth-century empress dominating her uncouth boyars, or a twentieth-century peasant babushka inured to cold and hunger, war and oppression. I've only just consciously realised, as I began writing these notes, that she wasn't Russian at all. She was the daughter of an English merchant living in St Petersburg and a mother of German descent. Half English, half German – and more Russian than any Russian.

This was how she ran the School – like a Russian matriarch, on her own terms. She was said to have imposed her own conditions on the War Department before she agreed to set it up. She refused, first of all, to teach anyone wearing a uniform. So, before we got anywhere near Cambridge, we all had to be taken to the Army Demobilisation Centre at Woking and turned back into civilians. The taxpayer having paid out only a couple of months beforehand to costume us in khaki and air force blue, he was now charged to dress us in a demob suit and all the regular demob trimmings – shirts two; collars two; collar-studs and braces; shoes and socks; underwear and rainwear; a choice of trilby hat or flat cap.

She also had her own understanding of what the School's functions were, and the training of Russian linguists was only one of them. She also saw it as an employment opportunity and support system for all the impoverished White Russian émigrés she knew, and all the Soviet refugees (two groups as dissimilar as different races, even in the way they spoke the language they were teaching us).

That was one of the most Russian things about her – her generosity and loyalty to her friends. She shared her house with one of them, Doris Mudie, who was destitute, frail, subject to nervous breakdowns, and nearly blind. When, much later, Lisa went to teach for a couple of years at an American university, it was said to be in order to pay the costs of Doris's medical care. For the time being, though, she had managed to get her on the payroll at Station Avenue with all the others, even though she wasn't a Russian and didn't know the language. She sat in a little room at the School with one of the suitcase-sized reel-to-reel tape recorders that were beginning to be available then, bent low over it to see the controls with her failing eyesight. One by one we were taken out of class and sent to her so that she could record us reading a passage from a Russian novel and then play it back to us. I'm not sure what pedagogic purpose this served, except to demonstrate even more graphically what we already knew – how remarkably unlike Russians we spoke Russian.

It was difficult to combine the charitable functions of the Slavonic Department with the scholarly ones more usual in an academic institution. Her successor in the chair, Anthony Cross, told me that there had been a moment of panic at the time when the Conservative government of the day was attempting to make universities more like businesses by imposing a hard-nosed regime of targets and measurable results on them. Lisa was informed that henceforth government finance would depend upon the number of publications by members of the faculty. The annual total up to then was said to be running at a very healthy zero. Lisa summoned everyone in the department to a crisis meeting. 'One of us has to publish something!' she told them, I imagine with all her usual urgent energy, and no doubt repeating it in Russian for greater emphasis. Stunned silence from the faculty. The only response, apparently, was from

Edward Sands. Sands, an Englishman who was the Russian tutor in my own college, had a reputation for sardonic offensiveness (he asked me, characteristically, how much I had paid the college for my honorary fellowship), and *had* once actually published something, so Cross discovered when he investigated – a children's edition of a Pushkin novella. 'After you, Professor,' said Sands.

Lisa no doubt brushed the suggestion away as dismissively as if it had been a grammatical solecism from one of us on the Russian course. Somehow the department survived its shortfall in scholarly product, and on she swept in life. At the age of eighty-four she at last found time for a diversion she had never tried before: marriage. Her bridegroom was a Serbian baron, possibly a few years younger than herself, whose manner suggested wide estates and armies of rack-rented peasants to toil on them, but who was probably one more of her charity cases. Eleven years later, when she was ninety-five, she was still game for yet another new adventure in life: she divorced him.

For her ninetieth birthday celebrations many people whose lives she had touched assembled in Cambridge to honour her. She must have outlived most of her old colleagues and fellow émigrés – even a fair proportion of her former pupils – but there were still a lot of us left to pay our respects, many of us who had used our Russian as translators and Slavists, journalists and diplomats. There was also a large contingent who arrived and departed together in unmarked buses – intelligence staff from GCHQ in Cheltenham.

The last time I saw her, at a dinner party near Cambridge a couple of years later, her eyes were just as bright, the immense forcefulness and energy just as overwhelming. Some time after midnight she excused herself. She had to get up at six, she explained, to catch the bus to London to do a full day's work at the British Library.

She died at the age of ninety-six. Not even this stopped her completely, because three years later, with the help of an editor, she at last took up Edward Sands's challenge and published her memoirs.

My Manchester Guardian

Another friend who first entered my life at Cambridge. Another one, too, who was a presence in the mythology before he was in the flesh. Another old Etonian, with the same real goodness that they all so improbably seemed to be blessed with. But in other ways remarkably unlike the others. Or anyone else I've ever met. Neal Ascherson.

He was a couple of years ahead of me, and he'd gone down long before I had a chance to meet him. Still hanging in the air, though, like the afterglow in a fluorescent tube, was the radiance of his reputation. A double-starred first, and according to his tutor in King's, the historian Eric Hobsbawm, perhaps the most brilliant student he had ever taught. He had become a legend even before he got to Cambridge. He had done his national service as an officer in the Royal Marines, fought in the Malayan jungle, where Britain was trying to suppress a Communist insurrection, and seen action. Many years later I read that he nursed a private anguish because he had killed someone out there. I don't know the circumstances – he never mentioned it – but it lent him a touch of dark glamour.

Actually he had become a legend even before his exploits in Malaya – when he was still at Eton. He was said to have stabbed another boy and been publicly flogged for it. I once tried to ask him what exactly had happened, but he didn't want to talk about it, any more than he did about his experiences in Malaya. One of the rewards of writing this piece was that when he read it he did tell me some of the details. He had carried out the attack not with a clasp-knife, as I had always believed, but a Moroccan dagger. And the punishment had been not a flogging but a ceremonial birching, carried out by the headmaster wearing his canonical gown and bands, in the presence of two witnesses known as praepostors, with a bundle of freshly picked birch twigs tied together with twine (and a spare bundle to hand in case the first one broke). 'Much less painful', he claimed, 'than caning' (by his fagmaster, Douglas Hurd, the future foreign secretary, better known in the school at the time as Hitler Hurd), 'but drew quite a bit of blood. I had to kneel on an eighteenth-century blackened oak block, and be held down by a college servant sitting astride my neck . . . Ah, what privileges I enjoyed.'

And then one day this legendary figure was suddenly, dramatically closer. The girl I was pursuing at the time told me that he had called on her in Newnham. He had been in the college visiting a cousin of hers and had taken the opportunity to tap on her door and introduce himself. It was like some kind of visitation from another world. 'I went weak at the knees,' she said, still trying to recover by laughing at herself. I felt overawed even at second hand, like the girl in the song who had danced with a man who had danced with a girl who had danced with the Prince of Wales.

Then, at the very end of my last year, he came to see *me*. With what I would discover was a characteristic taste for the modestly unassuming, he arranged to meet me in a spartan snack bar mostly frequented by people waiting for buses in Market Square. He turned out to be as powerful a presence as his reputation suggested – darkly handsome, with a touch of noble melancholy, and a quiet intensity that seemed to suggest depths of serious experience. Perhaps that killing in the jungle, or the stabbing and birching at school, had left their mark. He could have been a romantic hero out of a nineteenth-century novel, and his steely Scots crispness of speech suggested a background in the stormy wilds of Caledonia.

But this is too solemn. He would sometimes suddenly open his eyes very wide, half turn his head and look at you a little sideways with questioning irony, then laugh at the ridiculousness of things. And he was wearing army surplus trousers, apparently left over from his army service, camouflaged in the startling patchwork of colours of what I took to be the Malayan jungle.

Perhaps the most immediately striking thing about him, though, was an intense . . . *manliness*. It had nothing to do with any kind of swaggering or braggadocio. Quite the contrary; he was quiet-mannered and gentle, with, as I was to discover over the months that followed, a tender-hearted concern for others. He didn't need to demonstrate being a man – he simply *was* one. I saw why my girlfriend had buckled at the knees.

His meeting me was a manifestation of his generosity and thoughtfulness. He was working in Manchester, for what was then still called the *Manchester Guardian*, and he had come all the way down to Cambridge to introduce himself to me because he had heard that I was about to join the paper. Did I have any friends in Manchester, he asked me, who could help me with the practicalities of where to stay when I arrived and finding somewhere to live? I did not. 'Don't worry about anything,' he said. 'I'll look after it.'

And he did. He started by booking me into the Barcombe Hotel, in suburban Fallowfield, where he lived himself. It was a seedy establishment, even less assuming than the snack bar, but with a certain reputation among journalists and other bohemian riff-raff, and I should never have found it by myself. It was pulled down many years ago now, rather sadly, because it had been built by the young Alfred Waterhouse, the great Victorian architect, for himself and his bride when he was newly married and working for Manchester Corporation, designing the extravagantly Gothic town hall that has been the city's logo ever since. The heads of Waterhouse and his bride still gazed touchingly at each other from the dining-room corbels above the bleary-eyed breakfasters. But the place had declined, like Manchester itself at that time, and it had an atmosphere of gloom and leaking coal gas, while Manchester's copious rains maintained a lake in the yard that made getting to some of the rooms like an expedition through primeval wetlands.

A lot of people who knew Neal's background must have been caught out by his profound unposhness, my father for one. He had driven me and my bags up to Manchester to start my new life, so I took him out for a drink with my one acquaintance in the city, preparing him in advance by listing the salient points in Neal's CV. My father did his best not to let me down with my new upper-class friends. 'Belong to any clubs?' he asked Neal grandly. Neal looked surprised. 'The Blue Orchid,' he said. 'The Beefsteak?' queried my father, who was very deaf. 'The Cavalry Club?' 'Just the Blue Orchid,' said Neal – an establishment, as I discovered later, where the local journalists went to drink after the pubs had shut.

I grew a little restless with what seemed to me the slightly excessive unpretentiousness of the Barcombe Hotel, and Neal, even though he was perfectly happy there himself, said he would help me find somewhere where the gas and water flowed a little less freely. Which part of the city did I want to live in? he asked. I'd no idea.

'Just show me the artists' quarter,' I said, a suggestion that gave me a certain instant celebrity in the city. Wherever I went thereafter, as soon as people heard my name they would start to laugh. 'You're the man who asked for the artists' quarter!' they cried happily. 'In Manchester!'

The implausibility of an artists' quarter at that time was the kind of thing Neal liked about the place. It was of a piece with the easy-going friendliness of the people. 'If you're on the bus home on a Saturday night and you're too drunk to stay awake,' he told me, 'you don't need to worry. Someone will always say, "Just tell us where you want to get off, love, and we'll see you right."' He took me and my problems on in rather the same spirit, spending hours patiently walking round the artist-free streets with me, looking for somewhere that might meet my approval. I remember we talked a lot as we walked, but not what it was about. Consciousness, Neal tells me now. Why, he apparently wanted me to tell him, since I was supposed to be a philosopher by training, was he looking out of his eyes and not mine? I was very scornful, he recalls, and said it was a non-question. Which was a fashionably positivistic way of dealing with it, in the style of the times, but I now think it was one of those unprofessionally formulated puzzles that could have led us into a lot of interesting exploration.

He also told me everything I needed to know about the world I was entering and the life I was embarking upon. I confessed to him that I was very uncertain whether I was going to be up to the work as a reporter; in spite of all my efforts since I got the job, I still hadn't been able to bring my shorthand up to a usable speed. That wouldn't matter, he assured me. The reporters on our rival papers viewed the *Guardian* staff with the same soft-hearted indulgence as the passengers on the buses did the Saturday-night drunks. They didn't see us as representing any serious professional opposition, and they showed their respect for the paper's reputation by taking it upon themselves to *fill us in* after press conferences from their own notes. I told him, more flippantly, that I also had a problem with punctuality. 'Ah,' he said seriously, 'that *will* matter.' He turned out to be right on both counts.

He claimed to be taken by the excessive unassumingness of a trilby hat we saw in the window of a run-down gents' outfitters in Cheetham Hill. I urged him, satirically, to buy it if he liked it so much, and affected, perhaps to get my own back for the art-ists' quarter, to attribute his reluctance to his Scots carefulness with money. We were way down the street by this time, but he at once went back and bought it. He may even have worn it occasionally thereafter, to justify the expense, though mostly, so far as I recall, he kept it in the office together with a pair of fur-lined flying boots in which he had concealed a bottle of Scotch, all on standby for covering stories which might involve blizzard conditions.

It was his identification with the Scots that was the enduring focus of his passionate romantic idealism. He later extended it to embrace the Poles, another fiery people who had been repeatedly walked over by their more powerful neighbours. He learned the language and got beaten up so badly by a mob in Warsaw, appar-ently at the instigation of the political police to discourage him from interviewing dissidents, that he was in hospital there for a long time. In 1968, by which time he was the *Observer*'s corre-spondent in Germany, it was the idealism of the emerging German student movement that attracted his sympathy. He had all the scep-tical journalist's suspicion of authority, but also – not always the case with journalists – a really serious empathy with the oppressed and struggling.

This had already complicated his career on the *Guardian* before I arrived. He had been taken on in the first place not as a reporter but a leader-writer, and his area of special interest was to be the struggle for independence then being conducted by the peoples of Britain's imperial possessions. Most especially those in Africa, where he had been travelling after he left Cambridge, and where his outspoken sympathy for the aspirations of Black Africans had outraged the local Whites and forced him to seek sanctuary with the governor of Uganda, Sir Andrew Cohen, by good fortune like Neal a member of the Cambridge Apostles. The *Guardian* fully shared Neal's passionate belief that Britain should get out of Africa, but it envisaged our withdrawal as a gradual and carefully managed process while the indigenous populations were prepared for self-government. Neal believed we should get out *now*, today, preferably before teatime. The differences were too extreme to bridge, and he was moved out of the Corridor, the oak-panelled cloister from which the leader-writers told the world what it should be like, to the Room, the rather scruffier junior common room where we reporters told it, more modestly, how it presently was.

But (a characteristic *Guardian* compromise) he was still *paid* as a leader-writer. If I recall right, I was on twelve pounds a week and he was on twenty. His lifestyle was so unassuming, though, that the reckless generosity of this income, as it seemed to me, didn't mean much to him. We got our wages in cash every Friday, like the printers and foundrymen, in a blue envelope, always urgently awaited. One day, while we were sitting in his room at the Barcombe, he happened to feel in the pocket of an old raincoat hanging behind

85

the door, and brought out an unopened blue envelope that must have been lying there forgotten for some weeks. Twenty pounds short and he'd never even noticed! I didn't know which I found more impressive, his wealth or his frugality.

We both moved on, I to the *Guardian*'s London office, he to the *Scotsman*. I rather lost touch with him, until a few years later we found ourselves together again on the *Observer*, where he turned out, as he had on the Corridor in Manchester, to be a little more radical than they had bargained for. Every now and then the National Union of Journalists would ask me why there was no union chapel at the *Observer*. I was semi-detached from the office by this time, so I would pass the query on to my page editor there, and he would tell me that we didn't need a chapel at the *Observer* because we were all gentlemen together. This seemed a reasonable answer to me, but Neal evidently took a different view, because eventually he helped found a chapel, and inspired everyone to behave less like gentlemen and more like trade unionists.

He went on to a career as a journalist and historian of great brilliance and amazing range. He knew so much! Large things and small things, past and present, across the whole range of Europe and beyond. In the 1980s he began writing a column in the *Observer* that gave him a chance to explore all these interests, in pieces later collected under the title *Games With Shadows*. I've just been re-reading some of them; they're so well informed, so well written, so deeply engaging. He wrote some of the scripts for Thames Television's gigantic history *The World at War*, and became a frequent contributor to the two most intellectually serious publications of the English-speaking world, the *New York Review of Books* and the *London Review of Books*. He also wrote a masterpiece, *Black*

Sea, which focussed a huge range of history, geography, autobiography and even hydrography by following the voyage his father had made in 1920 as a young midshipman aboard one of the British battleships sent to rescue the remains of General Denikin's White Russian army from Novorossiysk. And in his eighties he began a new career as a novelist, with *The Death of the Fronsac*, which contrives to unite his two great themes through the story of the Polish Division in Scotland during the Second World War.

What never changed were his extraordinary quiet charisma or the generosity of his character. When, twenty-five or so years after my spell in Manchester, one of my daughters, just out of college in her turn, got a work placement on the *Observer*, he endeavoured to make her at home there just as he had me on the *Guardian*. And long before that he was helping me again. Not with accommodation this time, but, when I went to write some articles about Berlin and Vienna, with the contacts he had made when he had been the paper's correspondent in Germany. Which I suppose is about the most generous thing that one journalist can do for another, and which turned out to change my life.

I'm not sure what I've ever managed to do for him in return. Apart from persuading him to buy a hat he didn't want.

Berlin Blue

'Sarah Haffner?'

'Yes?' says the small, cautious voice at the other end of the phone.

I've just arrived in Berlin. I have to explain to this faceless voice that I'm here to write something for the *Observer*, and that a mutual friend has suggested calling her. The friend is Neal Ascherson, who used to live in Berlin when he was the paper's correspondent here. Sarah will tell me what's going on, says Neal. She's a painter; she knows everyone in leftish artistic and literary circles, and everyone knows her. Also she was very involved in the student movement that swept Germany in 1968, four years earlier, and changed so much here. She's the person to talk to.

I hate making these opening phone calls when I arrive in some strange place to write about it. People have better things to do with their time than talk to some ignorant journalist who's been wished upon them. You can hear their hearts sinking at the prospect.

'Neal suggested I should call you,' I begin – and the word is magic. At once all the anticipated difficulties are over.

'Neal?' she says in a very different voice. 'Oh. Do you want to come round? Now, if you like. Where are you?'

It's 1972, and where I am is almost halfway through my life. I don't know it yet, but everything is about to change. I've hardly ever been to Germany before, but for the next half-century I'm going to find myself coming back to it over and over again, writing articles, plays and novels that touch on German subjects, trying to improve my grasp of the language, making German friends, talking to German readers and theatregoers who turn out to have a welcome propensity, by no means universally shared, for reading my books and seeing my plays.

I suppose everyone needs a somewhere else in their life – a place that isn't home, that can offer the possibilities of romantic otherness that we all crave. For some of my German friends it's England, implausible as it seems to me, or some particular corner of it where they once came when they were young – where they fell in love with some local girl, perhaps, and that they go back to now and then, half hoping to see her coming down the street towards them. For me, when I was seventeen, and it was first possible to set foot in the great world beyond the English Channel that had been closed off by the Second World War, it had been France and Italy. I can still feel the transforming strangeness of them, but everyone else has long since loved them into familiarity. In the 1970s, though, relatively few of us have yet set foot in Germany. Why should we want to? Everyone knows there's nothing good to eat there, and nothing to see except nothing.

So, as I begin my travels around Germany, it's a bit like rediscovering a lost treasure. One of the things that piques the imagination, I have to recognise, is knowing what horrors have been committed here and what destruction has been wreaked. And, then again, to see how, unbelievably, it's possible to recover from those scarcely imaginable depths. There's something, too, about the whole style of Germany that feels right to me. The combination of restraint and *Gemütlichkeit*, of warmth and seriousness. The surviving glories of the past, but also the sheer craftsmanlike solidity of even the most utilitarian post-war rebuilding. The kindness of Germans towards strangers, and their supposedly non-existent sense of humour. Something in the air of especially North Germany – Hamburg, Lübeck, the North Sea and Baltic coasts, the landscapes and townscapes animated by Mann, Storm and Fontane. And Berlin, which is where for me it all begins.

Well, of course. It's June. The lime trees are coming into flower and are scenting the famously good Berlin air with their impossible sweetness. The streets are softened by the snowdrifts of white fluff from the poplars. Who wouldn't be charmed? Particularly by the Western half of the city, in 1972 still islanded deep inside the Democratic Republic, surrounded like a secret garden by the Wall and the still disputed and unreclaimed wastelands left by the Second World War. Part of its enchantment is the challenge it offers at every turn to make sense of what you're seeing. What's it *for*, this great capital with nowhere to be capital of? Why is it maintained at such vast expense, this great industrial complex without a hinterland to serve? Why is there a city here at all in the first place, for that matter, in the sandy heathlands of the Mark Brandenburg, far from sea, mineral ores or coal?

In fact all the contacts I have managed to assemble in the city will turn out to be easy and friendly, relaxed and welcoming – part of a whole generation that has abandoned the formality and stiffness of its forebears wholesale. So perhaps Berlin would have captured me and changed my life anyway, even without Sarah.

• • •

She lives in Charlottenburg, the district of quiet, discreetly wealthy streets around the Kurfürstendamm, which in those days, long before the fall of the Wall, is the axis of the city's commercial life, entertainment and vice. The heavy mansion blocks date from the vast prosperity that was released by the Franco-Prussian War. They have been thinned out and knocked about by the last war, but patched up, cleaned and repainted, and supplemented by sleek modern commercial buildings. Here and there authentic Wilhelmine doorways and entablatures complicate the smoothed-out facades. There is an air of unpretentious and peaceful stylishness.

Sarah's own street, the Uhlandstrasse, is a bit more knocked about than most, a bit more modest and serviceable. The everyday ordinariness of the shops is one of the things she likes about it, I discover later – the butchers and cleaners, the pet shop and hardware store, the House of a Thousand Hats, and the shop that sells lingerie for the fuller figure – 'the stronger lady', as Germans say. Her own block is authentically old Berlin, with a street door opened by a double-headed 'Berlin key' that you have to pass right through the lock, then retrieve and turn on the other side, and that leads to the sequence of sunless courtyards where so many Berliners, rich and poor, have always lived. I can't remember how far back her own court is, only that it's filled by the traditional chestnut tree, which forms the view from the no less traditional 'Berlin room' in the L-shaped corner of her flat.

I'm going to get to know the interior of that flat rather well in the months and years to come, because the walls are covered with her paintings, a lot of which, like so many painters' pictures, are of the interior in which they are hanging – some of them showing other pictures of the flat that are already on the walls. Here is a painting of the bookcase, every title legible – and there is the bookcase itself, with the same titles. Here are the loo and the bath; there are their images, even more boldly definite than the originals – more loo-like

and bath-like. Here is the table she works at – and there is the picture of it, with the morning sunlight filtering through the blinds,
waiting for her to start her day's work painting the picture. And
then in this picture is the painter herself, stretched prone on the
chaise longue, resting after she has painted it. There she is again –
and again – often thoughtful or melancholy, and done in shades of
blue – the colour she always returns to. In one of them she is looking questioningly out of the frame with a caption asking anyone
looking back, 'Who am I, who are you?'

And there, amid all the painted Sarahs, is the living original. A
slight but wiry figure, with shining, dark, dramatically kohled eyes.
Short, dark, wiry hair, with a small splash of white in the front of
it like a soldier's cap-badge or a fox's flash. Painter's clothes: old
trousers, scruffy sweater. Disconcertingly, casually prettier than she
is in any of her self-portraits. But her manner is forthright and challenging, and even when she's smiling she's watching you to see how
you're taking it. You feel she's used to having her fists up, and the
way she doggedly hunches her shoulders as she walks suggests that
life has not been entirely easy.

Which it hasn't. This flat in the Uhlandstrasse, she says in a
memoir she wrote many years later, is the only place she has ever felt
at home. She moved into it on her twenty-first birthday in 1961,
when it was still wrecked by war damage, and the first paint she
applied was not to a canvas but to the flat itself, mostly in various
shades of the blue that recurs in her pictures, and suggests an under-
current of loneliness and mournfulness running deep in her in spite
of all her pluck. She says in her memoir that she has always felt herself to be an '*Außenseiterin und Zuschauerin*' in Berlin – an outsider
and looker-on. In one of the earlier and most striking self-portraits

95

she is standing at the big window in the Berlin room, a slight and suddenly vulnerable figure, turned away from us, looking out over the chestnut tree and the world on the other side of the glass. The allusion is to the famous picture by Caspar David Friedrich of his young wife looking out at Dresden in the 1820s. Friedrich's observer, though, is gazing into a world full of promise, and she is being lovingly watched in her turn by the unseen husband behind the easel. Sarah Haffner's young self is looking out at a much bleaker world, from a much bleaker standpoint – divorced, and a single mother, watching alone, and being watched and recorded by no one but herself. The light outside the window is going at the end of the day, and the dusk is tinged with that melancholy blue of hers.

She is an outsider twice over. She was born and brought up in emigration, in England. Her father is Sebastian Haffner, the journalist and historian, who had to leave Berlin in 1938 because his wife, Sarah's mother, was Jewish. He was a lawyer in those days, called Raimund Pretzel. 'Sebastian Haffner' is the *nom de guerre* he took, half from Bach and half from Mozart, for the sake of relatives still in Germany during the war. His daughter was called Margaret, as any English schoolgirl might be. Then, when she was fourteen, her father decided to move the family back to Berlin. Margaret found herself dumped in a school that seems to have made little allowance for her knowing no German, and she had to learn it as best she could as she went along. She was homesick for years. She once famously told an interviewer that she was 'one and a half people – half German, half English, and half Jewish, in that order'. She swapped 'Margaret' for 'Sarah' as a kind of *nom de guerre* of her own, because it was the name that the Nazis forced on all Jewish women alike to obliterate their individuality.

Outsiders are often the sharpest observers; they notice all the things that insiders have become accommodated to. The Berlin of the thirties was famously captured by a visiting English writer, and Sarah said that over the years she had read Isherwood's *Goodbye to Berlin* seven times. Adolph Menzel, the greatest painter of Berlin, who recorded its development into a *Weltstadt* in the nineteenth century, was born in the provinces (Breslau – now Wrocław, and part of Poland), and moved with his family to Berlin at exactly the same age as Sarah Haffner did. Maybe it's because she learned German as an outsider that she sees its virtues so sharply. 'It's such a beautiful, expressive, sturdy language,' she tells me in a letter years later, to encourage me in my efforts to improve my own grasp of it, 'like a sculpture hewn out of a block of wood. Even the weather forecast sounds like a poem: *Anfangs neblig-trübe, später diesig, nach-mittags vorwiegend heiter, gelegentlich leicht bewölkt.*' And maybe, too, it's why she comes to write both languages so well, with the same clarity and directness as she paints.

She spends the rest of her life in this same flat in the Uhlandstrasse. In time, though, she extends her range, from the small domestic details that give her such security and pleasure, to the street outside and the district around it. Gradually the great alien metropolis becomes, as she says in her memoir, *her* city. And not just as the subject of her paintings. From her student days this secret outsider is involved in everything that's going on around her – the art politics of the fifties and the student movement of the sixties, the dreary work of union organisation and citizens' initiatives. When, later, a wife in one of the other flats in her block who has been beaten up by her husband comes knocking on her door late at night begging for sanctuary, she not only takes her in but starts a movement to set up hostels for all the other battered wives of the city.

Of *her* city; but she regards it with the same sharpness as she paints it. Where I see, as we walk around in the weeks to come, the sunshine and the easy life of the pavement cafés, she sees a hidden world of embittered war widows and ex-Nazis. She overhears an old woman whispering to her friend about her: 'One of the cinders that slipped through the oven grating.' The radical left had seemed to offer so much hope in 1968. Now, she says, it's broken up into disunity and impotence. 'Everyone's either smoking pot or going SEW.' The SEW is the Western counterpart of the SED (East German Socialist Unity Party), authoritarian, controlled by Moscow like the rest of the great, unfriendly empire that surrounds this little island. She has no sympathy with the party, but keeps up friendships in the eastern half of the city, even though getting through the checkpoints to visit is so time-consuming. She claims actually to like the enervating grey inertia of the Democratic Republic – its sense of time suspended, the bone-shaking setts in the roads and the scabied yellow stucco of the houses that survive like dreams lingering from the night. 'It's much nicer walking round East Berlin,' she says. 'It's like Berlin used to be, without all this silver paper added.' I can't help liking the silver paper – the neon signs, the car washes, the second-hand Mercedes for sale along the kerb of the Kurfürstendamm, the softly glowing restaurant terraces. She gives little scornful laughs if I risk saying so. *Quatsch* – nonsense – is a word that I become very familiar with.

She sees me, I realise, with something of the same scepticism as she sees the city. I'm thirty-nine. She is looking down from the more secure ground of thirty-two. 'Have you had your mid-life crisis yet?'

she asks. I laugh; I haven't, and have no intention of trying anything so banal.

'You will,' she says.

She turns out to be right. I will. I *am*. This is it, starting now, here in Berlin with her, as we speak.

• • •

I get beyond it, though, in time, with a good deal of anguish for everyone involved, and I finally manage to put together a slightly wary friendship with her that lasts for another thirty years, though it's always coloured by the memory of what it once was, and that always requires a certain amount of mutual tact. We come to maintain a correspondence that sometimes flares up, then dies away again for months at a time. She listens to a lot of music, and we exchange suggestions for CDs, sometimes the CDs themselves. Whenever I'm in Berlin we have lunch together, walk around Charlottenburg, go to galleries. She loyally comes to the Berlin first nights of my plays and the talks I give when a so-called reading tour for one of my books takes me there. She learns to drive, improbably, and our excursions are extended to poignant suburban cemeteries she has discovered, or, on sunny summer days, further out into the Mark, to try the new season's famous white Beelitz asparagus. I continue to have romantic feelings about the city; she continues to find them *Quatsch*.

Her relations with her father become more and more difficult, and cast a darker and darker cloud over her life. But she and her son remain close, and when he marries and has children they give her great joy. She goes to look after them in Dresden; they come to stay with her in Berlin. Her work seems to be going well. She has a lot of exhibitions and sells a lot of pictures. She has so much work in hand, and some of it on such a large scale, that she breaks out from the flat in the Uhlandstrasse and rents a studio on an industrial estate in Moabit.

In art, as in other things, she has always been an outsider. Representative art, when she was a student at the College of the Arts in Berlin, had been usurped by abstract expressionism. She married a fellow student, Andreas Brandt, whose own paintings, she says in her memoir, were at that time becoming ever more abstract. She was painting in the same style herself, but after a visit to the 1962 Venice Biennale, where in one pavilion after another there was only more of the same, she decided that this conception of art was uniform to the point of tedium, and she separated from both it and her husband. She went back to depicting the real world – but found a way of using the formalism she had learned as a way of distancing herself from the subject.

Within two years of leaving the college she wrote herself a private manifesto in which she formally recorded her understanding that art derived from the conflict between object and abstraction. So this is what she goes on to do – she simplifies, isolates, and makes everything more boldly and more expressively itself. She does it most dramatically of all with colour. In a lot of her pictures she reduces the city to a few rectilinear outlines – and then creates its life at each time of the day and each season of the year by the changing gradations in the colour of the light washing over it. The blue end of the spectrum remains her home key. Pale winter blues, deep summer blues. The blue of the morning, of the afternoon, of evening and night. Blues used to transmute the skin tones of faces and torsos. Melancholy blues.

The city, *her* city, with or without the silver paper, becomes her great subject. It's not by any means her only subject, any more than it was of Menzel in the previous century; but like Menzel she returns to it again and again, and like him gives it a particular individual character. What she shows, and what I slowly come to see through her eyes, is an astringent mixture of the ghostly old and the bleak new. In some of her pictures there are glimpses into Wilhelmine staircases and doorways; but more often she paints the shifting urban sunlight catching the featureless geometry of the new high-rise buildings, or the concrete service towers emerging from blank construction sites, or that even more characteristic feature of Berlin – the vast pale windowless walls of apartment blocks chopped in half to excise bomb damage, or to let light into dark *Hinterhöfe*. She paints the tumbled gravestones in overgrown cemeteries, the lonely old women looking out of the windows of their isolated apartments, and the young drug addicts collapsed on the pavement.

She gives my wife and myself three of her prints. We've had them on our walls for nearly twenty years now and the more I see them the more I like them. She helps me a lot over the years, particularly with my German. She explains the complex conventions for *Sie* and *Du*, and advises me which of my German friends ought to be which. She teaches me a number of the colloquial usages that give spoken German its savour: *Kuddelmuddel*, for the hotchpotch it sounds like; *Schnickschnack* as another of many ways of saying *Quatsch*; *doppelt gemoppelt* for tautologously saying the same thing twice over, like this. She goes on having a bit of a soft spot for the old Democratic Republic long after it's collapsed, and is amused by the way some East German styles and usages are infiltrating the West, as with the *Ampelmännchen*, the little man on the traffic lights who tells pedestrians when to wait and when to go. In the West he has always walked, in an orderly and careful way, as he does in most places in the world. One of the little quirks of East Germany was that he ran, a rather endearingly self-important figure in a hat. Now, by popular demand, he is starting to run on West Berlin traffic lights as well – and not *ruck-zuck*, the way people used to do things sharpish there in the past, but *ratz-fatz*, the way they did them in the East. She is delighted to find, in some small town she is visiting in the East, that things are *tote Hose*, dead trousers. I'm not sure whether that's an Eastern usage as well, but it's the perfect expression for the way pretty much everything in the East once used to be.

As my German improves she helps me even more by making it the language that we write to each other in. She checks the odd bits of German that some of my characters use. When I write a play about German politics she tells me exactly what I need to read to start my researches. For one of my novels I need to know if you can find privet in the suburbs of Berlin. She spends hours driving round Zehlendorf and Nikolassee to check. When my German publishers propose to call another of my novels *Das verschollene Bild* (The Missing Picture), I phone her to ask if it isn't a bit, well . . . *dull* . . . She laughs. 'It's *extremely* dull,' she says. 'Exactly the kind of title we like in Germany.'

She comes with her son to see us in London, and with some difficulty we find the old primary school she went to, where she had a teacher called Mr Fremantle, whom she credits for teaching her to write. ('When you have written a sentence,' he told her, 'look to see if you can't cross out one or two words, and when you have written a paragraph if you can't cross out one or two sentences.') There's not much else I can do for her in return for all her help, either linguistically or professionally, except to write the foreword to her memoirs. And that she rather balances out by writing a contribution to a *Festschrift* published by German academics for my eightieth birthday. In it she claims that I did once actually manage to do something useful for her. It was in 1990, in the strange and exhilarating months after the crossings between East and West Berlin had been so astonishingly opened at last, when people were beginning to break the Wall up into building rubble and souvenirs. We were in the Adalbertstrasse, in Kreuzberg, a cul-de-sac, closed off by the Wall. But there in front of us, as unlikely as a tear in the whole fabric of reality, was one of the new home-made holes that had started to appear. So we went through it . . . and we were in no-man's-land, the death zone of raked sand where you were either killed by a mantrap or shot on sight by the border guards. In the second wall that closed the zone off on the other side was another rough-hewn hole in the world. We went through this one in its turn . . . and suddenly, impossibly, like children in a story who go through the back of a wardrobe and find themselves in some secret other world, we're in what's visibly East Berlin. And here's the oddest thing: that, here in East Berlin, we're still in the Adalbertstrasse.

'I was numbed,' says Sarah in her essay.

It was the moment when it came home to me in a wave of emotion so strong I felt it physically, that this was one city and that it was reunited. It was also the moment when I felt deeply that this was my city . . . I had seen people dancing on the Wall and falling into each other's arms at the Brandenburg Gate. I was happy with them, but as an outsider . . . I always felt like an observer rather than a participant, and in those days this feeling had been enhanced. It had taken an old friend from England and showing him what was going on to make me realise that this was my city . . .

This moment of mine as the outsider's outsider is probably the high point of our friendship, in fact, because the year after she writes this something goes wrong between us. For no reason that I can make sense of she says she is having painful flashbacks of the past and doesn't want to continue our correspondence. It's so sudden and inexplicable, and her recollection of events is so confused, that I can't help wondering if it's a late after-effect of the concussion she suffered a few years earlier after a fall from her bicycle. The doctors hadn't been able to find any trace of damage on her brain scan, but her son tells me later that she developed Alzheimer's, which can sometimes be caused by a head injury. Or perhaps the intermittent sadness that has always lurked just over the horizon of her life has simply closed in, like the dusk of that long-gone winter's day outside the courtyard window of her flat.

I never see her or hear from her again. Someone tells me that she has withdrawn into herself and no longer goes out of the flat that has been her refuge for so long. But seven years go by before any more definite news arrives. Which is that she has died.

I look through all the volumes and catalogues of her paintings that I have. They are her life, and it continues beyond her death. There she is still, looking back at me out of her blue world. There is the flat in the Uhlandstrasse, with the morning sunlight on the desk where she will work, and herself looking out at us, sometimes sadly, sometimes thoughtfully or questioningly, or just stretched out on the chaise longue, tired at the end of her working day. There are the streets of Berlin, *her* city, in all the changing seasons and times of day. And, hanging on our walls, the three prints she gave us: the solid Berliner with a briefcase going wearily away from us up the long blue-windowed stairs of Gleisdreieck U-Bahn station; the famous black cat streaking towards us down a blue-treaded Charlottenburg staircase like her own; a sunlit rape field somewhere out in the Mark. The rape field is brilliant yellow; but, now I look at it, I see there are dark blue hedges behind the yellow, waiting for summer to end.

Absent Friend

I am a believer. Not in disembodied beings who might kill your enemies for you if you ask them nicely enough, or in schemes for having a good time after you're dead. All that kind of thing is a bit beyond even my credulity. Nor in the fictions that modern politicians have found to be such acceptable substitutes for facts, which I'm too out-of-date to appreciate. I've even, after a number of chastening experiences, got a little cautious about people you meet who just need a few pounds to get home to Sidcup, or acquaintances who email to say their wallet has been stolen in Bucharest, or plain-clothes policemen who want to take your bank card away for forensic examination. But friends who for some reason get pleasure out of finding someone they can make a fool of not for financial gain but just for its own sake, just for fun – I'm their man. I have given a lot of pleasure to quite a number of them over the years. I'm not sure what this tells me about myself. A craven-hearted desire to please? A sensitive appreciation of fiction that has been one of the sources of my professional career? Or plain stupidity?

One of the people I obliged most handsomely was the actor David Burke, who was playing the Danish physicist Niels Bohr in the original production of my play *Copenhagen*, and whose transparent guilelessness made him the perfect casting for the famously sweet-natured Bohr. It also, I discovered only later, made him the perfect casting for an apparently simple-minded but unfortunately fictitious lady called Celia, who wrote to me to say that she had found a cache of secret papers relating to the Nazi atomic bomb programme under her floorboards. David made such a total fool of me that all I could do to put a good face on it was to write a book about it with him, so I won't rehearse the embarrassing details again here. It turned out that he was a regular hoaxer. He did something similar in every production he was in, he told me, and he always found someone to believe him. My distinction was to believe a story even more preposterous and more elaborate than any of his other victims, and to go on believing it for longer, in the teeth of even more conclusive evidence to the contrary.

He only fooled me once, though, whereas another compulsive deceiver of my acquaintance called John Sackur did it over and over again. One of his stunts had a considerable effect on my career – a beneficent one, as it happens – which is why I've included him here.

He was in my college at Cambridge, and he was perhaps the most distinguished of all my contemporaries there. He was tall, athletic and handsome, like the clean-cut hero of an old-fashioned adventure story, and he had a quick mind and a sardonic sense of humour. The college's numerous sportsmen liked him; so did its handful of alienated intellectuals. But the most striking thing about him was that he was a compulsive dissembler. He loved deception for its own sake, and never ceased to be amused by the endless credulity of his victims. One of whom was me.

We were all rather in awe of him because he had spent his national service as a front-line infantry officer in Korea . . . Though, even as I write that, it occurs to me to wonder how I knew. He certainly wouldn't have told me himself. He never boasted. That wasn't his style at all. Quite the contrary. He would have told me that he had spent his time, like so many other national servicemen, performing fatuous military routines in some dull camp in England. He would have laughed ruefully, and I would have sympathised, since I'd had a rather better time, and I would have found out the truth only later, then felt a fool. Once again. He appeared in Hall in the last few days before Finals struggling to get through what I knew was his first-year reading list. He was rather desperate, he said – he hadn't done any work for the last three years and he was trying to catch up in a week. He laughed ruefully, and this time I could tell from the particularly rueful way he laughed that he was telling the truth. He got a first, of course.

And joined the Foreign Service, where he would have cut a wonderfully dashing figure in his various overseas postings. Not that it helped him make much headway in the service. I ran into him once or twice over the years, and he laughed ruefully about his lack of success. I was a little cautious in my sympathy, until one day I ran into him in the street and realised that this time he really was in a bad way. His marriage had broken down, he told me; he had lost everything in the divorce and he was living in lodgings so squalid that he was ashamed to give me the address. He was so embarrassed about it that I didn't like to press him. Which was just as well, because a mutual friend to whom I passed on the sad news told me that it was in fact an apartment in Albany, the famously exclusive enclave in Piccadilly.

I can't remember now whether it was before or after this that he asked me for my help. He was totally disillusioned with the Foreign Service, he told me, and wanted to get into journalism instead. Did I know anyone in the business? On the *Sunday Times*, for instance? I did; I knew the editor, the great Harold Evans. Well, John was an outstandingly intelligent and able man, with an inside knowledge of many different parts of the world, so I suggested to Harry (with many warnings about John's deviousness) that he might be worth interviewing for a job on their foreign staff.

The next time I saw Harry he was a lot less friendly than usual. He had followed my suggestion, he told me, and invited John to come in and talk to him. But he had also invited Frank Giles, the foreign editor. The conversation had not gone very far when Frank, who had previously worked in intelligence, suddenly said, 'You're a Friend, aren't you?' John confessed that he was, and Harry had to explain to me that Friends were what the employees of MI6 called each other.

So it wasn't the Foreign Service that John had been working for all these years. He was a spy. Of course. What else? How could he not have been? In normal circumstances Harry might not have found this little deception too surprising or difficult to accept. But I was working at the time for the *Observer*, the *Sunday Times*'s great rival, and our Beirut correspondent, Kim Philby, had just fled to Moscow, unmasked as one of the so-called Cambridge Spies. The paper had found it embarrassing enough that he had been working for British intelligence, never mind Soviet intelligence as well. Harry had jumped to the conclusion that I had been trying to compromise and embarrass the *Sunday Times* in their turn.

I've only just discovered, in the course of writing this, that Harry describes the episode himself in his tumultuous memoirs, *My Paper Chase*. He says he found John a mystery. Was he really motivated, as he claimed, by his dissent from the government's failure to suppress white supremacism in Africa? The conversation seems to have become interesting when Harry mentioned Philby. John revealed that he had been tasked with writing a report on Philby and the damage he had done, and Harry recalls him as dropping a series of intriguing hints about it. So did he perhaps represent a group of rebels in the service who thought that the purge after Philby's unmasking had not gone far enough? Or were his indiscretions 'cunning bait to suggest he was disaffected enough to be a genuine defector whose integrity could be trusted'? Harry seems to have been in two minds. He agrees that he accused me of foisting a spy on him. At the same time, though, 'recalling the intensity of expression on [John's] chalk-white face, as he expounded on foreign policy at our first meeting, a lunch at the Ivy, I am inclined to conclude that he was not a plant, but a young man whose conscience would give him no rest'.

In fact I recall Harry as saying, though he doesn't mention this in his book, that he did offer John various possible postings as a foreign correspondent, but that John turned them all down (no doubt with a rueful laugh), because they were places where the KGB could have got at him and assassinated him. His hints about Philby, though, seem to have been helpful in the big investigation of the affair that the *Sunday Times* subsequently undertook, and I suspect that John probably continued to supply them with material. Perhaps this was what he was really up to – leaking (with my obliging assistance) the version of the story that MI6 wanted to make public. Who knows?

I had long before this started writing novels. Perhaps it amused John to know privately that we were now both purveying fiction for a living, though I suppose in my case with rather less danger of getting assassinated. And perhaps I never told him that I'd found out what he'd been up to all his life, because it was falling for yet another of his deceits that gave me the idea for one of mine, and helped get me going with a new sort of untruths – plays. I should have thanked him, and I don't think I ever did. He died young, of a particularly horrible disease that somehow suggests bottling things up inside oneself, and maybe it was before I'd had the chance.

And I suspect there were things to bottle up. I did just once see him at a moment of genuine vulnerability. It was in college. Something happened at breakfast. I can't remember now what it was. I think he brought a letter in and opened it, then went out, looking so stricken that I followed him to see what the trouble was. I found him in his room, weeping; the girl he was in love with had dumped him. I made him some coffee, he gradually got control of himself, and neither of us ever referred to the incident again.

So here, belatedly, is my account of what I need to be grateful for.

My college and I had not been on the best of terms, and I had departed without leaving a forwarding address for fund-raising appeals, the college magazine, invitations to reunions, etc. So I should never have discovered that my particular year was due for its Gathering of Old Members if John hadn't rung me up and told me. He suggested that we should go to it together. I was very reluctant. It would surely be a pretty dreadful occasion, I said. He laughed. Yes, he agreed, it would.

'But it would be nice to meet up and have a chance to talk,' he said. 'We could sit on the sidelines, have a certain amount to drink and a good laugh at the whole occasion.'

In the end I allowed myself to be persuaded. He got the college to send me an invitation, and I went.

He didn't.

So I had the certain amount to drink that he had suggested, but not the good laugh to go with it. Next morning I walked round Cambridge with the worst hangover since the invention of alcohol, while he sat, presumably, on some rather more remote sidelines enjoying the good laugh. At me.

Here, though, is what I have to be grateful to him for: that in the fullness of time a (highly fictionalised) version of that evening became *Donkeys' Years*, my first commercially successful play. And not only did he provide me with its setting but with one of the characters – a (no less highly fictionalised) version of himself. He is the man with the mysterious and colourful career, the man that nobody knows much about, the man that everybody, sportsmen and intellectuals alike, is really looking forward to seeing again at the reunion.

He has another quality, too, that as his author I can't help privately finding rather attractive. Casting a play is often tantalisingly difficult for everyone involved. This particular character, though, never gives us any trouble at all, because, after all the anticipation, he fails to appear.

Five Minutes Fast

The first thing you see of any new country, as you emerge from customs at the airport, is a long line of the local citizens watching you.

They're taxi drivers and limousine chauffeurs, or the representatives of tour companies, and they're holding up cards with people's names on them. Perhaps one of them has a card with your name on it. Or perhaps none of them does. You'd recognise your own name if you saw it, of course. But the people holding the names up are at a disadvantage. They won't recognise you. They won't know whether it's you or whether it's somebody else. If they did they wouldn't need to hold up a sign.

For years now, every time I've emerged from customs somewhere and seen that line waiting, I've had the same thought. Supposing I went up to one of them who was holding up a name that wasn't mine, and claimed that it was. If I'd stepped through this waiting door into someone else's life. Just to see what kind of world would begin to open up in front of me. How I'd cope. How far I'd get before I was found out.

I'd never really do it. I'm far too timid and law-abiding and set in my ways. Then a few years ago my wife and I went on holiday to a Greek island, and there once again was the usual crowd of waiting drivers and name cards. Only this time, for some reason, I suddenly remembered a man I'd once known who was severely manic-depressive. When he was down, like the grand old Duke of York, he was down. But when he was up he was not just at the top of the hill like the Duke, but a mile above it. You never knew what he was going to do next. He didn't know himself. Something would come into his head out of nowhere and at once he'd do it.

He once told me that he'd found himself walking along a London street with heavy traffic moving at walking pace beside him. Keeping pace with him he saw there was a Rolls-Royce with white ribbons on the bonnet. In the back sat a young man in a morning suit and a young woman in a wedding dress. At once my friend knew what they wanted him to do: to get into the car beside them and entertain them. So he did.

His name was John Gale and he'd died thirty years before my arrival on that Greek island. If John Gale had been there instead of me, I thought, and the idea of claiming to be someone else had happened to fall into his head, he'd have done it. And from this brief and unheralded reappearance out of the past sprang the idea of having a fictitious character do the same, and seeing what would happen. The idea for a novel, in other words.

Which I then wrote. So John Gale is another of the many people I am professionally indebted to.

I already was, as it happens, long before this – long before I ever met him. He was one of the two reporters I most admired and longed to emulate when I was a student and had ambitions to be a journalist. The other was James Cameron, the famous roving correspondent on the *News Chronicle*. Cameron I actually set eyes on. I was visiting the *Chronicle*'s offices on a vacation job interpreting for a delegation of Soviet students. There, pacing impatiently up and down the newsroom, was Cameron, romantically handsome and coolly, casually elegant. He had his hands on his hips and looked as darkly louring as a summer thunderstorm, in the middle of either creative agonies or a row with the management. When I did finally get to be a professional journalist myself, and was earning enough at last, I tried to imitate his style of dressing. I can't remember making any effort to copy the dramatics, though – or his writing.

The model I did attempt to imitate I had never seen, or even attempted to imagine. He was the converse of Cameron, a disembodied presence, without appearance or character, that manifested itself only through what he wrote – and it was his writing, not his personality, that had the effect on me. The only newspaper that I or my friends at university ever read was the *Observer* on Sunday. For most of us its greatest attraction was probably Kenneth Tynan, its modish and flaunting drama critic, or perhaps Paul Jennings, its eagerly whimsical humorous columnist. For me, though, it was John Gale, the paper's star descriptive reporter. How I would have characterised *him* in a couple of words, I couldn't have told you.

This was in the 1950s, and there was a fashion at the time for what was called the offbeat. Cool jazz, oblique cartoons, spindle-legged chairs left over from the Festival of Britain, wispy 'mobiles' (not phones then, of course, but hierarchies of dangling bits and pieces like three-dimensional family trees mapping relationships that shifted with every breath of air) – anything that seemed to catch life lightly and casually, in a minor key, on the unstressed notes of the bar. And in journalism the master of the offbeat was John Gale.

What did he write about? I can't now recall precisely: odd characters, disjointed social occasions and traditions left stranded by the tide – the overlooked dusty corners of life. He saw them all as if for the first time, with a sharp but coolly innocent eye, devoid of malice or judgement, explanation or interpretation, and he described what he saw with a deceptive simplicity and apparent naivety, as if he took the world at its own valuation and was letting it describe itself. His speciality was the inconsequential detail, the oblique but revealing remark. He himself remained invisible, a wryly amused ghost, so that I felt I knew him only as one knows oneself, the ever-present absence from one's own experience. When I started work as a reporter myself, on the old *Manchester Guardian*, I tried to emulate him. With only mixed success. The inconsequential in my hands remained inconsequential. It was harder to be John Gale than I had imagined.

I met him finally when I joined the staff of the *Observer* a few years later. Whatever he had turned out to be like in the flesh would no doubt have come as a surprise, but the actual reality was difficult to take in. He was not an absence at all, but a powerfully idiosyncratic presence. There was something oddly anomalous about him. He had a thatch of young man's fair hair that went with a kind of youthful eagerness and awkwardness of manner, but sorted oddly with a face eroded by anxiety and the weather of life. He had been a Guards officer during the war and he had an accent to match, but his style of dressing – untidy corduroy, woollen shirts, and I think a louche teddy-bear overcoat – suggested something more raffish and bohemian. He laughed and teased a lot, but the laughter was sometimes a little too relentless, the teasing a little too pressing, and his eyes remained anxiously watchful. His eyes, yes . . . There was something about them that you wanted to describe as hunted, or perhaps haunted.

For good reason, as I soon found out: he was severely manic-depressive. Everyone on the paper knew how his burgeoning career as an overseas reporter had been cut short by a wild delusional breakdown while he was in America, perhaps triggered by a previous assignment covering the brutal efforts of the French to retain Algeria as a colony. He would tell you about it himself, with disconcerting frankness and unsettling laughter, watching to see how you took it. I'm not sure, though, that any of us suspected quite *how* odd and fractured his world was, and always had been, until in 1965 he published his quite extraordinary memoir, *Clean Young Englishman*, in which he reports on his own life with the same apparent innocence and naivety as he did on the rest of the world, with a vivid immediacy undistorted by explanation or interpretation. His dramatically shifting moods affect everything. 'When I am manic,' he writes in the (manic) prologue to the book, 'I am close on six feet tall; when I am depressed I am not much over five feet ten inches. If I am manic, my watch gains five minutes a week; if I am depressed it loses five minutes a week. When I am manic my beard and finger nails grow faster. In depression, my hair lies down; when I am manic it stands up electrically, catching sensations like antennae.'

Perhaps it was this heightened receptivity in his manically charged hair that made him such a good writer. When his hair was up, though, and his watch was running fast, he became an unguided missile. Some sudden notion would come crackling out of the ether and he would act upon it. He recounts in the book how, as a newly commissioned young officer in the Brigade, he was already being inspired to invite the future queen to dance a foxtrot with him, even though he had never danced in his life before. By the end of the book, shortly before he is taken off to a clinic for residential care, he is borrowing a pneumatic drill off the foreman in charge of roadworks in a busy London street, and attempting to dig a ditch across it to bring all the traffic to a stop.

I don't think I ever saw the real depression, or the extremes of the mania, but even his everyday levels of the latter could be alarming. I'd written a novel about the newspaper industry, with a character who had something in common with an unsuspecting colleague of ours on the paper, and John would adapt some of the more extravagant lines of his dialogue – 'Oh, Michael, you write like an angel!' etc. – to perform to me in front of the original, in the latter's excitably gushing manner. And he would observe me as he did so with those watchful eyes to see if he had managed to embarrass me, then laugh his disconcerting laugh when he saw that he had succeeded.

When I was talking at a literary festival many years later about the later novel that John had inspired in his turn, I told the story of how he had got into the wedding car. His brother was in the audience, I discovered afterwards, and he told me that I had only got half the story. John had stayed with the couple, he said, and gone to the wedding with them, where he had joined the receiving line and shaken all the guests' hands, then made a speech at the wedding breakfast. Which had apparently gone down very well.

Re-reading his memoir reminds me how little I had ever got his measure, even when we were colleagues together. I can't remember now how I first heard the news of his death, some nine years later. But when I took in the details – drowned in a stream on Hampstead Heath, apparently incapacitated by the pills he had taken to kill himself – I understood at any rate one thing: that, even after I had borrowed his style for my reporting, and something of his reckless unpredictability for the character in my novel, I had never really understood anything about him.

Going Round

In the late 1960s, when I was thirty-five or so, the relatively even tenor of my life began to change, as if the wind were gradually swinging round to a new quarter and leaving a different season in the air. There were a number of things that contributed to this, and one of them is an event I can date exactly: Saturday, 5 October 1968.

I was living with Gill, my first wife, and our three young children in Blackheath, in South-East London. The bald plain of playing fields on the heath itself, and the trees of Greenwich Park beyond the gates that opened off it, were a celebrated oasis of green in the dour grey boroughs around. It was a social oasis, too – a colony of solid professional-class families that had moved there for the greenery, and also for the chance to live in the elegant seventeenth- and eighteenth-century houses, cheaper than their equivalents in West London, that had clustered around the royal coat-tails of Greenwich Palace, or for the ingeniously landscaped estates of sharply designed small houses that the developer Span and their architect Eric Lyons had annexed to them. It was six miles from central London, with no Tube – and rather more than six miles from all the social and cultural innovations that those years have become famous for, though the wife of one of our neighbours was famously the mistress of another neighbour's husband, which made us all feel a bit more in touch with the modern world.

I liked it. I liked the grass and the trees, and I found our neighbours, mostly people much like ourselves – Spock and Span, as someone called us – rather congenial, even the straightforwardly monogamous ones. You need neighbours in life. They don't have to be friends, just people you're friendly with, which is rather different. People you can stop and chat with – people you feel you could, as the phrase goes, borrow a cup of sugar from – perhaps with children the same age as your children, who might invite yours round to play, even to stay.

Among the neighbours, anyway, we had a social circle, some fellow Spanners, some rather more Georgian, and we all dinner-partied back and forth, agreeably enough. One of the more distinguished members of our circle was Richard Ollard, the historian, very much a scholar and a gentleman – also, rather improbably, my editor at my then publishers, Collins. In 1968 he and his wife sold their large, solid, Edwardian house, which had never seemed quite historically or architecturally distinguished enough for them, and bought one of the notably more elegant and suitable Georgian houses on the opposite side of the road. With characteristic social grace he took the trouble to introduce his incoming purchasers to a few of their future neighbours, Gill and me among them. Which is how, over drinks on that Saturday evening in October 1968, we first met Peter Nichols and his wife Thelma.

They turned out to be remarkably unlike the Ollards, or us, or indeed any of our other neighbours. In the first place Peter was newly famous. He had just had a huge success, in both London and New York, with his play *A Day in the Death of Joe Egg*. It had made him not only famous but rich, which had enabled him to throw up his job as a schoolteacher, leave behind their native Bristol and all the hard struggles they had had in life, come to London, and buy this large house in the most famous street of leafy Blackheath. Fame and wealth! Not quite what we were used to in Blackheath, particularly new fame and new wealth, the kind of thing that pop stars and footballers went in for. Then again, they were both rather . . . vivid. They were *characters*, and their life together as a couple seemed more like something in a comedy series than anything we were used to in Blackheath.

We took to them at once, and they to us. They became, yes, friends, certainly our closest in the district, and transformed it for us.

Peter's background was actually not entirely unlike mine. His father was a rep for the Co-op; mine for a building materials manufacturer. He had been to his local grammar school; I had been to mine. We were both writers by trade, we were both inclined towards comedy, and we apparently looked alike, though we could never see it ourselves: thin, bony, specs, prominent chin, high forehead. Over the following years I was complimented so many times on Peter's plays that I gave up demurring, and simply accepted all the tributes as gracefully as only someone who hadn't earned them could.

But there the similarity ended. Peter's life had followed a different course – not university, journalism and the metropolis, but training college, teaching and the provinces. He was a natural comic performer, and his great skill was mimicry. He mimicked the theatre people he worked with, his parents and Bristol relations, and soon his new neighbours in Blackheath, including me, I think, when I wasn't there to see it. He caught some thread of life deep in all of us, seized it, and made comic characters of us. Like a lot of comedians, though, he was at heart a pessimist, and wonderfully able not to enjoy things, such as his new-found success. The corners of his mouth would turn down at any reasonable opportunity, he would sigh heavily and his shoulders would slump. What he recalled mostly of his triumph in New York was being put down by a barman for his polite English diffidence: 'Could I have a glass of beer?' – 'You look old enough.' His closest friend was a fellow play-wright, Charles Wood. The two of them maintained a campaign of comic resentment of the greater professional success they felt that Tom Stoppard always seemed to be having; like a lot of comedy, it was not entirely comic.

Writing was a kind of addiction for him. He wrote every day, including holidays and Christmas, whether he had anything to write about or not. Outside his study, though, he left all the work to his wife. It was Thelma who had to have all the ideas, make all the decisions and get everything done; he mostly limited his role to complaining about the result. This was not the Spock and Span style at all. We liked to share all our domestic tasks. Or believe we did.

Thelma, yes. Peter's entire life depended on her. She was Welsh, the daughter of a Swansea builder, boldly attractive like a flaring dark poppy. She spoke with the same comfortable Bristol accent as the characters in Peter's plays, and the same comfortably casual syntax. Which was not the way we spoke in Blackheath – nor the way Peter did himself, for that matter. She was always smiling and pleased to see you, always eager to do things and ready to laugh – then suddenly incapacitated by glooms that matched his. She was a painter – a good painter – and their house was full of family portraits she had done, some of which caught Peter's melancholy intelligence with a sharp intelligence of her own. But her career had been systematically blighted. When she was a girl her father had refused to allow her to take up a scholarship to study in Paris, and now she had escaped from her father's tyranny she had fallen under Peter's. His endless demands for attention left her with little time to pursue her talent. Did she mind? Yes, she did! Or did she? It was hard to know. She complained, vociferously, but she was proud of him and his success – and proud of how difficult he was. She got great pleasure from laughing about him, and herself, and their strange, unfair relationship.

Everyone loved Thelma. I suppose even Peter, though they both claimed never to have been in love with each other. One of the things she had to do for him was to enjoy his success for him, and spend their new-found wealth on his behalf. Firstly on the new house, and soon a second one in France, on clothes and presents and works of art. Their three children were about the same ages as our three, and they stuck with the local primary school out of polit-ical loyalty; but now they had live-in nursemaids and au pairs. She was Mrs Newly-Rich; it lifted your heart to see the delight that she got out of their release from the constraints of the past, in a way he never seemed to manage.

What both united and divided them more profoundly than any-thing else was the tragedy of their firstborn, Abigail, who was not with the three at home in Blackheath, but in a home of a different sort. She had been born after a labour of long-drawn-out suffering, and, as they had slowly been forced to realise, had no normal cog-nitive function at all – no ability to communicate, no ability even to give any sign of recognising them, or anyone or anything else in the world. She was the terrible and arbitrary burden they bore in life – and she was also the source of all their wealth, because she is the subject of the harrowingly comic play that had established Peter's reputation. Bri and Sheila, the parents in the play, are Peter and Thelma, or comic projections of them. Joe Egg is Abigail (all she can do, as Bri's mother says of anyone left idle, is 'sit there like Joe Egg'), brought on stage to confront and shock us (in the teeth of objections from the Lord Chamberlain, the theatrical censor of the day, who wished to spare us our anguish), inert apart from giving the occasional whimper and soiling herself. Her parents live out the impossible dilemma that the child sets the world – the extreme archetype of the endless confrontations that occur in life between reason and emotion, between common sense and common feeling. Bri deals with the situation by recognising what he sees as the harsh objective reality: that she isn't a human being in any sense that can make social or moral demands upon others. He has hardened his heart to mock the lingering impossibility that Sheila feels to give up her love for the child she has borne, her never quite extinguished hope that Joe might somehow improve, her longing to find some trace of sentient life to cherish. What is so shocking about the play is that it treats their dilemma not as tragedy but as comedy, the source of embarrassment and social difficulty for everyone who is drawn into the story.

The brutal brilliance of Peter's work Gill and I discovered only later. While the play was running in the West End she had been pregnant, and we had been warned that it would terrify us. The warning came from a surprising source – the wife of Joe Melia, the actor playing Bri. Actors and their partners don't usually warn off potential customers, but when we did eventually see a production we understood what she had meant, and I think we both felt that perhaps she had been right.

Peter and Thelma talked to us about Abigail, of course, with the frankness they talked about everything, with which Peter wrote about everything. Maybe, though, the fact that we hadn't actually experienced the graphic harshness of the play helped us to escape from the subject and enjoy their new life with them. Which we did. We went to Bristol with them, met Peter's family, and saw the city through his eyes. We went to Mumbles, to stay with Thelma's aunt, as she so often had as a girl. We drove down to Périgord with them in family convoy, to see the derelict old schoolhouse they had bought and to translate for them their negotiations with the local craftsmen who were to bring it back to life. Peter and I played tennis and squash together, both pleased to have found a partner bad enough. We began piano lessons with a young Czech refugee who had arrived in Blackheath after the so-called Prague Spring, and were both even worse at it than we were at the games. As Christmas approached we were packed off to the West End, where I was instructed to take Peter out for a good lunch of the sort that chaps are supposed to enjoy together, with a few glasses of wine to cheer him up – and not to come back until I had persuaded him to buy some reasonably expensive piece of jewellery for Thelma, so that she wouldn't be embarrassed at the family Christmas party, as she normally was, by his having failed to get a present for her.

So they changed our life in Blackheath for us. What had the most profound and lasting effect on me, though, was the introduction that knowing Peter gave me to the world of the theatre.

I had spent the first dozen years of my professional life despising it; sour grapes, I'm afraid, after the failure of a revue I had written at university. A number of the newspaper columns I'd written since had mocked the theatre – particularly the embarrassment of waiting for actors to forget their lines or drop their props, and the artificiality of the plays they were performing even when everything went right. I had in fact been softening a little even before I met Peter. I'd had a couple of television plays produced, and for a variety of reasons found myself writing a handful of short entertainments for the theatre. But seeing it now through Peter's eyes was one of the things that encouraged me to launch out wholeheartedly into the form that was going to become half of my late professional life and provide most of my professional income.

I suppose in the first place it was really what one can only call the glamour of Peter's success that beguiled me. He was on easy social terms with famous actors and actresses, film directors and New York producers. The routine of his writing life was enlivened by the excitements of casting and rehearsals, of rows and betrayals, of first-night nerves so bad that he had to take tranquillisers to endure them. He introduced me to the theatre's engagingly absurd private lore and practices. First-night presents and camp first-night wishes ('A warm hand on your opening!'); never uttering the name of the Scottish play, on pain of being sent out of an actor's dressing room to turn round three times in the corridor; finding the pass door and 'going round' after the show, with ingenious camp ways of congratulating an actor whose performance was too terrible even to lie about (limp wrist, roguish smile and, 'What about *you*, then!'). Once again, as with so many of my friends in life, in so many different ways, he led and I followed. And followed as ineptly as usual, at any rate with the first few plays that I went on to write, which all failed most unglamorously.

We had missed *Joe Egg*, but he invited us to the first nights of two more successes – *The National Health* and *Forget-me-not Lane*. They made the playwright's life seem such a golden pathway. You wrote a play – it was produced – it was a hit. But this wasn't the only way that Peter had an effect on me. It was through him that I became friends with the two directors he had worked with most: Michael Blakemore, who did *Joe Egg* and the other two of his theatre plays that I saw, and Christopher Morahan, who did his precisely observed and wonderfully funny TV films. I went on later to work with both of them, to my incalculable advantage.

I also learned a few lessons from the plays themselves, and from what Peter told me about them. The theatre isn't bound to strive (unsuccessfully) for cinematic realism, I discovered, or to be solemn in order to be serious. Art, serious art, can be rooted in popular entertainment; *Joe Egg* itself had originated from a comic monologue that Peter had written for himself to perform. In *Joe Egg*, as in the monologue, Bri is a schoolteacher supervising a class in detention, the audience is the class, and Bri picks on them, mocking and nagging, almost as a music-hall comedian might. You could imagine that on some nights an audience might actually have stood up when they were told to and put their hands on their heads. Michael Blakemore (who evidently had as large a part in the success of *Joe Egg* as he did subsequently with my *Noises Off*) suggested extending the direct address from the opening monologue to the rest of the action. Peter learned the lesson, and passed it on. There the audience are, he told me, occupying most of the theatre, so you might as well recognise their existence and their part in the evening's proceedings.

And, when I at last actually saw the play, I understood something else about the audience: it's not only a participant in the action but the medium in which the emotional charge of the drama builds, like the electric charge inside a thundercloud, sometimes to be released as abruptly as a flash of lightning. One of the most shattering events ever in a play is the famous moment in *Joe Egg* at the end of Act One when, without any explanation, the brain-damaged Joe suddenly comes on stage playing a simple skipping game, like any child in the world, and tells the audience that it's the interval. Peter said that he hadn't foreseen the huge emotional impact that this apparently offhand reversal of the irreversible injustice of fate would have; he had put it in during rehearsals simply as a way of telling the audience that it was the end of the act.

This is what may have first made me think about the dynamics of the audience that I've written about elsewhere. There were other characteristics of Peter's work, though, that I could never have attempted to imitate. He told me once that he had never invented anything. He had simply recorded what he had seen and heard. I didn't take this quite literally, but it's true that his best plays were based closely on his own experience. *Forget-me-not Lane* was a portrait of his father; *Privates on Parade* came out of his improbable national service, touring the Far East with an entertainments unit; *The National Health* from another of his misfortunes, a long stay in hospital with a collapsed lung. The dialogue he gave his characters is probably too brilliantly idiosyncratic for any writer ever to have made up. His talent was to catch it on the wing and to fix it by mimicking it. He adapted it and intensified it – of course he did – and he did sometimes invent, but with mixed success. Where he was inimitable was in recreating himself and the people closest to him, most particularly his parents, Thelma and her parents, and making them speak as they spoke and act as they acted. I could only admire his skill. When I was writing fiction I occasionally borrowed a few details direct from life but, whatever unconscious memories a psychoanalyst might believe I was drawing upon, I need to feel that I am making everything up.

This difference is partly a moral one. To present yourself with complete honesty and no attempt at disguise takes courage. To do the same to the people around you, with whom you spend your life and with whom you expect to go on spending it, takes even more courage. And not just courage but an ability to anaesthetise your awareness of their feelings – the famous chip of ice in the heart that every writer is supposed to have. Even I have a last small melting fragment somewhere; Peter had enough to keep a turbot fresh. Thelma seemed to be happy to endure his mockery – her complaisance was one of his great resources. In any case she was such a sympathetic original that she survived the treatment pretty well, certainly in comparison to his depiction of himself. His father emerges from *Forget-me-not Lane* mostly as a comic character, but the picture of his life is painfully pathetic. His mother must have been suitably chastened to watch herself up there on stage and discover quite how cold-hearted and ignorant she was. You might wonder how Peter mollified her. The answer is that he didn't. He packed her off to see herself in one of them, I've forgotten which, with only the au pair for company. 'Oh, Peter!' she said to him when she got back, he told me later. 'I wasn't as bad as that! Was I?' And once again he caught her voice precisely. It sounded painfully wistful.

There were more plays, not all of them quite so good or quite so successful. Abigail died at last, at the age of ten. Thelma grieved; Peter refused to pretend. They were both liberated, and Blackheath didn't hold them long. In fact they turned out to be inveterate movers. First to Highbury – a grander house, with a famous conductor living next door, and a bit nearer the centre of London. Then to the middle of Shropshire, to get right away from London and the kind of people who live in Blackheath and Highbury. Closer to greenery and hills, and to John Osborne and his wife, who were also marooned up there, with nothing to do to keep themselves occupied but drink champagne. We rather lost touch with them, and the next time I saw Peter, a few years later, he seemed very depressed. It was their house that was getting them down, he said. 'All you can see out of every window is greenery and hills.' They came back to London, to a top-floor flat in Maida Vale. Why Maida Vale? Because . . . because at any rate it wasn't Shropshire. Or Highbury, or Bristol, or Blackheath.

Which of them is the driving force behind their moves? I imagine that they both have roles to play. Thelma, I suspect, enjoys being where they are, in spite of her occasional depressions, while Peter gets more and more discontented, and sighs, and lets his shoulders slump like an exhausted weightlifter dropping his weights, overcome by the unfairness of finding himself stuck wherever it now is. Thelma gets more and more impatient with him, and finally gives in and goes out to find somewhere else for them to live. And organises everything, yet again, while he complains about it. And finds yet another circle of neighbours for him to mock.

Now here I am, in spite of everything I've said to the contrary, being almost as sharp about him as he was about people. But then this isn't fiction – it's true! He *was* like that! And I hope I've made clear how much I admired him as a writer. At his best. Like a lot of people who are outstandingly good at something, though, he wanted to show he was good at other things as well. Plays that escaped the limitations of his own experience, and expanded to large political and historical themes. Novels, apparently, though I never read any of them and none was ever published. But the success that had deluged down on him so suddenly and richly ebbed slowly away. He didn't take it gracefully; his sourness about the injustice of his fate became notorious.

And then, somewhere in the middle of all this, he wrote *Passion Play*, and he was his old inimitable self again.

It's personal, like all his best work – intensely personal, the account of an affair he had had with the widow of one of their closest friends. Its format is as technically bold and idiosyncratic as *Joe Egg*, with the characters of himself and Thelma each split into two different selves and played by two different actors. It's lacer-atingly honest about the erotic pleasures of adultery and the price that has to be paid for them in humiliatingly squalid deceit. The mistress is allowed only one self and is perhaps more a projection of the man's imagination than a real person, even though she and all the circumstances of the affair seem to be drawn from life. But the wife, her trust betrayed by both husband and friend, is Thelma in all her vivid lovability, all her pain and humiliation, even to the suicide attempt with which she almost ends the long story of their life together.

Peter sent me the script before it was produced, because someone had suggested to him that I might think it was about me. It's true that my life had changed by this time. I was out of both Blackheath and my marriage, and some of the play's events, I had to recognise, were a little close to home. I was touched that Peter should be so uncharacteristically concerned about my feelings, particularly after we had been more or less out of contact for a number of years; maybe the producer was worried about legal action. I was happy to reassure Peter; the couple in the play, even divided four ways, were, as always, intensely and unmistakably Peter and Thelma. I was fairly casual about it, in fact. Reading it on the page I didn't really feel very disturbed by it. Only when I saw it actually played out as a dráma in real space and time did I find it so overwhelming. Another masterclass from Peter in how the true function of the writer's play is to make possible the actors' performances.

There is one way in which the play, like *Joe Egg* and *Chez Nous* before it, departs from life. At the end of *Joe Egg* Bri walks out of the marriage, abandoning Sheila to look after Abigail on her own without even telling her he is going. At the end of *Chez Nous* the Peter character is trying to break an egg, which I take to be the marital bond, but doing it lengthwise between thumb and forefinger and finding it harder than he imagined. At the end of *Passion Play* it's the wife who walks out of the marriage. Or at any rate half of her does. After the first production, as Peter records in his introduction, he changed his mind about which half it was that left and which remained (though the significance of the switch, as he also records, seems to have been obscure to most people – including, I confess, to me). Three plays that end with Peter and Thelma parting company, or contemplating it! Quite striking. In life, though, he never left her, nor she him. Were his stage personae living out an escape that he secretly longed for? He would surely never have survived the reality. Thelma might have, if she had been forced to, but Peter would have died of loneliness even if he hadn't died of hunger first. The nearest he ever came to trying it in practice was when he used to refuse, in their later years, to go to their house in France with her. Off she would defiantly go on her own – and then, after two days on *his* own, he would trail after her.

Looking at the list of his works before and after *Passion Play* I can't help feeling that his sourness was a little self-indulgent. He had had a success with *Privates on Parade*, based on his adventures on national service, providing old-fashioned concert-party entertainment to British troops in the jungle, which was funny in its mimicry of his fellow entertainers. In 1984 he published a good autobiography, with a title that combined his proclaimed sense of inferiority with one of his old camp show-biz jokes, *Feeling You're Behind*, and offers a picture of his father and the elaborately facetious character that he cultivated perhaps even better than the one in *Forget-me-not Lane*. *Joe Egg* was revived, and with such overwhelming effect that I felt obliged to find a phone-box (this was before mobiles) as soon as I had got out of the theatre and tell him so, even though we had pretty much lost touch by then, and even though I could still scarcely speak for emotion.

They moved (of course), still as restless as ever, and still as together. This time, even more oddly, it was to a top-floor flat in a new estate of the edges of North Oxford. Even more oddly still, this time they stayed.

Perhaps they had just finally run out of steam. Or perhaps they had at last found where they really wanted to be. It was certainly a delightful place, full of sunshine and Thelma's paintings, with huge terraces on the south and west as big as small gardens. He seemed to mellow a bit. They gave a notable party for Thelma's eightieth, when he was eighty-four, packing the rooms and terraces with their children and grandchildren, and with friends surviving from every decade of their long life together. Peter returned to his days as a performer, and read us a long verse tribute to Thelma that he had written, full of humour and affection. Perhaps something more than affection – love.

Love, yes. When I showed Thelma what I'd written about her

and Peter in this piece she said she didn't want to let what I'd said about their feelings for each other, or what I'd heard Peter claim about them, go unchallenged. 'I knew I loved him, and he knew it too, and said he couldn't love me because he didn't know what the word meant. The strange thing about it is that in the last month of his life he kept telling me he loved me and asking if I knew it. I think in his helplessness, which he really resented, he learned the meaning of the word "love".'

Finally. But he had grown very frail by then. I thought we might manage a rather dramatic reunion in 2019, when it turned out that we were having plays produced at the same time on opposite sides of Trafalgar Square – revivals of our two biggest hits, *Joe Egg* and *Noises Off.* I imagined us meeting halfway, among the fountains in the square, after our two curtains fell, and going for one of the cheering meals out together we had been prescribed all those years before. Or being at each other's first nights. Going round afterwards, saying all the right things, hugging all the men we knew in the business and kissing all the women, enjoying each other's success. He was past hugs and kisses, though – past success and failure. And by the time our two shows opened he was dead.

Magi

What is philosophy? Difficult to say, if you're not a philosopher by trade; even more difficult if you are. In its original usage it was relatively straightforward; it was from the Greek *philos sofos*, the love of wisdom. And at Cambridge, when I first began to study it, it still was. At any rate the Professor of Philosophy was much loved, and by some happy chance, or some whimsical inspiration of the faculty board who had appointed him, he was called John Wisdom.

In those quiet days in the middle of the twentieth century, to cast further confusion over the subject, the philosophy department at Cambridge was called the Moral Sciences faculty. Even people, inside or outside Cambridge, who thought they knew what philosophy was, didn't have much idea what Moral Sciences were. The faculty had had a distinguished history when Bertrand Russell and G. E. Moore had been teaching there, and had achieved its apogee under Wisdom's great predecessor in the Chair, Ludwig Wittgenstein. But by the time I arrived it had been overtaken in both size and influence by Oxford and various American universities. The subject was changing. It was becoming professionalised and technical, and it was harder than ever to know what it was and what it was for. A lot of it, it seems to me now, has come to exemplify what Richard Dawkins many years later called the Law of the Conservation of Obscurity, which states that 'obscurantism in an academic subject expands to fill the vacuum of its intrinsic simplicity'. At Cambridge, though, the old commonsensical British tradition of Locke and Hume, of Moore and late Wittgenstein, was still managing to survive. And its star was the professor, Wisdom himself.

He had been Wittgenstein's pupil, and one of the small group of acolytes to whom Wittgenstein had tried to confine his teachings. Wittgenstein – one of the greatest philosophers of the modern period, in my opinion still – had been a charismatic teacher with aspirations towards some kind of secular sainthood, who had tormented himself and everyone around him with his high-mindedness, and made their lives difficult by his awkward asceticism and imperious humility. He had required his college, Trinity, to feed him apart from the other dons, who vaunted themselves above their fellow men by dining on High Table, a few inches above the common herd. He wouldn't come to a college lecture room to teach; if you wanted to hear him you had to go to his rooms, and if you were self-indulgent enough to want to sit down you had to take your own chair. He forced his partner, Francis Skinner, to give up his research fellowship at Trinity in mathematics and take up more fittingly humble work in a factory. He had once refused to speak to Wisdom himself for several weeks because Wisdom had reverently shown some professional arcana, the notes he had taken down at dictation in Wittgenstein's lecture, to a fellow philosopher outside the inner circle. I am profoundly glad I arrived at Cambridge in time to benefit from the full flood of Wittgenstein's intellectual legacy, but three years too late to be in any danger of meeting him.

Wisdom was quite different – good-humoured, gentle, happy to lecture in a lecture room and eat on High Table, and not averse in general to the pleasures of college life – most particularly, I believe, the Trinity Foot Beagles. What he had inherited from Wittgenstein was his way of teaching, which was not lecturing in any usual sense, but actually *doing* the philosophy – conducting his thinking out loud – in front of the audience. The performance involved, as it had with Wittgenstein, a good deal of spontaneous dramatics. He would *get stuck* and be *unable to go on*. He would *ask for help*. Wittgenstein had apparently done this with notable pathos – and then impatient fury if anyone offered help he found unhelpful. He had once excluded Keynes from his lectures, like a disruptive schoolboy, for making an unhelpful suggestion. Wisdom was far too soft-hearted to reject any suggestions, however inept. But he made up for it by the rest of the performance: the dramatic suddenness with which he came to a halt in mid-sentence, the ringing slap with which he clapped his hand to his high bony forehead, the agony in which he screwed up his face, the prolonged hum of hesitation he sometimes uttered as he struggled, as if the cerebral machinery within were under such pressure that its working had become audible. A lot of people came from other faculties to watch in awe.

Quite what, if anything, the internal machinery was actually doing as it hummed was sometimes difficult to be sure of. An undergraduate I knew called Tim Green, who worked as Cambridge stringer for *Time* magazine, once came to see me to ask for my confidential advice. He had been asked by his editor, he said, to find out if Cambridge was pursuing a hot new philosophical technique, now apparently all the rage at Oxford, called individuation. The kind of problem it dealt with, the editor had told Tim, was this: if you had a man wrapped up in a blanket, how did you know it was the same man sticking out at both ends? It meant nothing to me (though I should have heard of individuation, if not of men wrapped in blankets). Why didn't Tim ask Wisdom, I said, since he was head of the department. 'I did,' said Tim. 'Of course I did. But he behaved in a rather funny way. I got the impression he was holding out on me. Do you think the Moral Sciences Department might be doing secret research for the Ministry of Defence?'

This seemed to me about as plausible as the possibility that it was planning to move to Mars, but Wisdom used to give an at-home each week to anyone who liked to drop in for coffee and informal philosophical chat, so at the next one I told him about Tim's suspicions and asked him what on earth he could have said to have aroused them. 'Ah, yes, Mr Green,' said Wisdom. He looked a little shifty. 'He came to me with some extraordinary story about a man wrapped up in a blanket. I couldn't understand a word of it. But he said they were working on it at Oxford and I didn't want him to think Cambridge was getting left behind, so I . . .' He made his long-drawn-out premonitory hum as he tried to find precisely the word to describe how he had finessed his answer, and leaned closer to confide it to me. 'I *hedged*,' he whispered slyly.

Wisdom did seem to be exactly what you might have hoped a philosopher to be like. The impression was reinforced by the implausible appropriateness of his name. Particularly since, even more implausibly, he had a cousin, also called Wisdom, and also a lecturer in philosophy. Another John Wisdom, in fact, though known in the business as J. O. to distinguish them, or perhaps to keep improbability within bounds. For there to be one philosopher called Wisdom may be regarded as felicitous; for there to be two looks like an upmarket game of Happy Families. Or else a contribution to the old philosophical question of whether the world determines language or language determines the world.

Whether J. O. Wisdom (who taught at the London School of

Economics – and was, I think, the philosopher to whom our own Wisdom had revealed the Wittgenstein esoterica) also got stuck in his lectures, and clutched his forehead, and asked for help, I don't know – I never heard him. Even if he did, he surely can't have done it as well as ours. One of the pauses ours made I recall particularly clearly, partly because it seemed as if it might never end, and partly because it was in itself an object lesson in philosophical method.

This wasn't in a lecture – it was at a meeting of the Philosophy of Science Club, where Wisdom was scheduled to respond to a paper read by a distinguished biologist. I can't remember what the subject was, only that I understood nothing of what the biologist said, and when I took a look around the audience at the end I had a suspicion that I was not the only one who was having trouble. But salvation was at hand, because Wisdom was rising to reply. He closed his eyes, as he so often did, tipped his head back, clapped his hand to his brow and screwed up his face in the familiar rictus of concentration. He was obviously going to take his time to get his response absolutely right, and then he was going to be authoritative, perhaps devastating.

We waited. A long time went by. There was not even the familiar hum that gave hope of speech being on the way.

In the end some of us could bear the tension no longer. One by one and two by two we began to slip away into the night.

At last Wisdom opened his eyes and took his hand away from his forehead.

'Would you mind repeating your main points?' he said humbly.

So that was what he had been doing all that time: summoning up the courage to admit that he hadn't understood any more than the rest of us. And that, it seemed to me when I began to try to do a little philosophy myself, many years later, is surely a good place to start.

Or, as Wittgenstein famously said at the end of the *Tractatus*: '*Wovon man nicht sprechen kann, darüber muß man schweigen.*' ('What we cannot speak about we must pass over in silence.')

• • •

There were one or two other notable performers in the faculty. Casimir Lewy, for instance, the fiery Polish logician who devoted a term-long course of lectures to a single sentence in a paper by Strawson. I think it was: '"A vixen is a female fox' is true" entails that a vixen is a female fox.' Lewy disagreed. Or Richard Braithwaite, who had married a student of his, Margaret Masterman, also a philosopher, but religious, and been obliged by her to get himself confirmed first. He had done it in Ely Cathedral, which was a public enough renunciation of his agnosticism, but was said to have been allowed by the Bishop to recite a version of the Creed that he had written himself, starting something like 'I believe that certain statements about a deity have a possible validity within the context of a particular discourse . . .'

Wisdom, though, remained the only member of the faculty who really caught my imagination. Until, in my last year, there came a new arrival, Wisdom's antithesis in every way, and who was going to have a lasting effect on my life.

It was ironical. I had first become interested in philosophy through reading Wittgenstein, and I was in exactly the right place to follow this up, because not only Wisdom but the whole department was still profoundly under his influence. But I had originally come up to Cambridge to read Modern Languages, and my college had only grudgingly let me change my subject. Whether this was reflected in their choice of the supervisor they found for me I don't know, but somehow they managed to hit upon the only member of the department who seemed to have remained untouched by the whole Wittgenstein era – or indeed by much else that had happened in the subject during the previous thirty or forty years. They also made him my director of studies, and since it's your director of studies who actually appoints your supervisor, it was to him I had to go, at the beginning of my last year, when I decided enough was enough, to ask him to unappoint himself and find me a different supervisor. I was as tactful as I could be. He had been an inspiration in every way, I implied, but it was really Wittgenstein I wanted to focus on, and I knew Wittgenstein was someone he wouldn't want to teach. I was right – he didn't. But apparently the only supervisor he could find who was free to replace himself was the new recruit to the faculty, Jonathan Bennett.

Jonathan turned out to be a pugnacious young man who had just arrived from New Zealand by way of Pennsylvania and Oxford. He was plainly rigorously intelligent and a born philosopher, but he was very wary of Cambridge's way of going about things, particularly of Wisdom's. It was difficult to imagine him *hedging*, or *getting stuck* and pitifully *asking for help*, or reciting some equivocal version of the Creed. He said very forthrightly – truculently even – what he thought and believed (he had some kind of downright nonconformist religious faith), and he was given to describing any views he dissented from as 'just plain wrong'. One of the things he was most resistant to was the teaching of Wittgenstein, particularly as refracted through some imprecise undergraduate enthusiasm like mine. So, after all my efforts, I was no better off than before.

Except that it didn't work out quite like that. Jonathan's combativeness meant that he loved to argue – a trait that I believe caused him some problems with his colleagues. It was difficult to say anything – particularly if it reflected the kind of Wittgensteinian ideas that almost anyone else in the faculty would have taken for granted – that he wouldn't immediately disagree with. My weekly supervision, at midday on Thursday, where I read him my week's essay, was gruelling. And at the end of it we would be so at odds with each other that we would be forced to retire to the pub next door and continue the argument over lunch. We would then occasionally go back to his room to argue all afternoon. It was impossible to defend myself against such an onslaught without finding out at any rate a little about what I was saying.

He could have knocked me out of the ring whenever he wanted to. But he didn't want to. Like an old-fashioned prizefighter who has private reasons to keep his opponent on his feet, he kept me on mine. It was his first year in the job; I can't imagine that he can have gone on maintaining this level of energy and commitment. Except that, in my case at any rate, he did, even long after I had ceased to be his student. We remained in touch, and whenever we met over the years in various parts of the world where he was teaching or doing a sabbatical we would continue to argue (for three whole days once, walking round San Francisco, when he was doing a year at Stanford). The question came up at some point about what made us happiest, and he said that he thought for him it was 'being in severe intellectual difficulties'. This, it seemed to me, was fair self-knowledge. He had become more intellectually

tolerant by this time – had come to understand what philosophers saw in Wittgenstein, certainly, and seemed surprised when
I reminded him how straitly religious he had been when I first
knew him. I remained always a little in awe of him all the same. I
think I had him at the back of my mind when I wrote *Copenhagen*,
and made Werner Heisenberg, on his way to see his revered old
mentor Niels Bohr, talk about the touch of fear one always feels
for a teacher.

We didn't always argue, of course. We also simply talked. He
knew a great deal about many things apart from philosophy, particularly music. When I was staying with him once during his years
as Professor of Philosophy at Syracuse he discovered to his astonishment that I had never managed to acquire a taste for Bruckner.
He at once improvised a simple but effective (and enjoyable) way to
teach me; he made me listen to the scherzos of three of the Bruckner
symphonies, one after the other. He had the first word processor I
had ever seen, and it was during the same stay that he introduced
me to this wonderful device that would change for ever the way
I worked. Once again he found the perfect teaching method. He
sat me down in front of the flickering green characters on the little
IBM screen, told me just enough to be able to start writing – and
left me alone all morning in his study to get on with it. When he
was in London he took me and my wife to hear Alfred Brendel for
the first time, and my children to see *West Side Story*. All in all he
was the living embodiment of what the Oxbridge tutorial system
can be at its best.

He gave me so much help in so many ways. He read the manuscript of a slim book I wrote on philosophical topics. Asking
professionals to help with the work of amateurs is a miserable

imposition, but he saw the best he could in it and saved me from some of the worst. Then, when it appeared, he went further and reviewed it as well – over-generously, but not uncritically. In fact he read many of my books over the years and his comments often seemed to me more perceptive than a lot of even the most favourable professional reviews.

He was plagued by tinnitus and he found the eighteen harsh upstate New York winters he spent in Syracuse increasingly difficult to bear. He retired to an island off Vancouver, but continued to work, and to help people understand philosophy, by making accessible versions of over a hundred texts of the so-called Early Modern Period, from Francis Bacon and Jeremy Bentham onwards. His wife Gillian, who radiated as steely an integrity and intelligence as Jonathan himself, began to suffer from dementia. She decided, as calmly and consciously as Jonathan himself would have done, and explaining her reasoning as clearly and coolly, to end her life, with Jonathan as her witness. He had been, she said in the rationale she published on the morning of her death, a husband beyond compare.

By this time he had performed another great service for me. I had written a second book on philosophical topics. It was a by no means slim volume this time, but he once again read it and saved me from many errors. I had borrowed rather freely from his work, and he offered many additional suggestions that made me look more knowledgeable than I was. His tolerance was even more striking than before. He had helped me make the best case I could for what I was arguing – then told me as frankly as ever how strongly he dissented from it. He didn't say, as he probably once would have done, that it was *just plain wrong* – though I could hear him thinking it, even off the west coast of Canada, seven time zones away – but, even more precisely devastating, that it was 'anthropocentrism run amok'. Which made me laugh. The old Jonathan, in spite of everything.

Pitchmaster

My long collaboration with Dennis Marks began in 1973, when I was already middle-aged and he was twenty-five and just starting out in life. There was this young producer, said my agent, who was making a film for BBC television about a personal passion of his, Laurence Sterne, and he was very keen for me to write and present it, because, on the evidence of my books and columns, he knew that I was a Sterne enthusiast too. Which I suppose I kind of was, I realised, now that this young man who didn't know me came to mention it, but which I hadn't quite realised up till then.

I was flattered, anyway, and it's only just occurred to me as I write this to wonder – since Dennis turned out never to have made a film before, and was simply one of the young hopefuls in Music and Arts fresh off the training course, with nothing on his CV yet but a first in English from Cambridge, still trying to get his career off the ground – whether he had actually already persuaded the BBC to let him do it. Or was he first persuading me that he had, and then, in the traditional way of producers conjuring something out of nothing, using me to persuade the BBC? Either way, it was a first demonstration of his skills at pitching, as they call it in the business, that in the following years were going to see us through seven more presented documentaries together, and him to the treacherous heights of the BBC's arts empire.

That first film was not such a big deal. It was only going to be fifteen minutes long, one of a series about famous writers made through the device of exploring the houses they had once lived in. We met in Kensington House, the now long demolished office block behind Shepherd's Bush, which looked like a run-down benefits office, but was in fact the palace where BBC Music and Arts pursued their byzantine politics, a world of plots and counter-plots in which Dennis seemed to be already entirely at home. He was a large, shaggy man, very clever, very eager and clumsy, who smoked importantly. He had the bushy black beard and student cap of a nineteenth-century Russian revolutionary, which went with a taste for the exhausting participatory workplace politics that the events of 1968 had made fashionable in the cultural world.

I re-read *Tristram Shandy* and drafted a script. We began to develop a pattern of collaboration, with him as producer/director and me as writer/presenter, that would be repeated over the seven full-length documentaries that were to come, with me putting forward half-thought-out ideas, and him suggesting tropes and devices to make them filmable. We had an enjoyable few days recceing the location, Sterne's old parsonage at Coxwold, in North Yorkshire. Then more work to make the script fit reality, followed by a few more agreeable days filming in the pale spring sunshine.

The presented documentary is an odd form of human communication, if you stop to think about it, with conventions as set and artificial as opera, but Dennis turned out, even on this first venture into it, to be confident and competent behind the camera. The old hands in BBC film units who had the technical skills and long years of experience with Arriflexes and Nagras, the cameras and sound-recorders of the day, and who found themselves working under directors fresh off the training scheme, sometimes took pleasure in making their young lives impossible, but Dennis was as persuasive

160

with them, and as able to win their allegiance, as he was with me and everyone else. And at the end of the working day, while the rest of us were sitting in the local pub with a drink, Dennis plunged back into the world of BBC politics and workers' control – shut away for hours in the pub's phone-box, participating long-distance in some interminable soviet going on back in Kensington House, emerging briefly at one point to ask hurriedly, without even time for persuasive flattery, if I would be the shop-floor candidate to front a new weekly arts programme.

I declined. But, as we finished the post-production on Sterne back in London, we decided to put up a proposal for a full-length presented documentary of our own about another shared interest – Berlin. It was a long shot; our joint credentials were that one brief essay about an eighteenth-century English parson. I didn't see Dennis pitching the project to Melvyn Bragg, who actually was now producing and fronting the new arts programme, and no doubt Dennis's skills were at least matched by Melvyn's noted generosity. One way or another, though, we found ourselves improbably entrusted with ninety minutes of prime air-time and a budget to match.

This was a much tougher proposition than Sterne. Our aim was to show Berlin not as it then was, the only too familiar divided Cold War battlefront, but as it had been in its heyday – to trace why there had ever been a great European capital in such an unlikely place. We obviously needed to film in both halves of the city – and the East German authorities, who didn't recognise the legitimacy of the Western sectors, had never knowingly allowed a film unit that was working in the West to work in the East as well. Persuading them must have been an even harsher test of Dennis's powers.

He managed it, though. We wrote our script and filmed all the locations in the West. Then, two days before we were due to make our unprecedented move across into the East, Dennis was suddenly faced with his greatest challenge yet. The East German authorities discovered that they had a long-standing total ban on the BBC because of a dispute over a bill that one of its producers had run up. The East Germans said it hadn't been paid. The BBC said it had.

It was (of course) the weekend. It was difficult to find anyone in either East Berlin or West London still at work. And in those days there was only a handful of phone lines between East and West Berlin, so interzonal phone communication was in any case almost impossible. We had spent two-thirds of our budget and we would have no film to show for it. Dennis made one wild attempt to persuade me to somehow rewrite the script before Monday morning so as to make it possible to film the whole thing in the West. Not even Dennis, though, could talk me into that.

By some extraordinary piece of detective work he discovered the source of the problem with the unpaid bill. It was for a country-house weekend – at Colditz, the fortress where the Nazis had held high-profile British POWs during the war, and which the BBC had made the setting for a drama series of the same name. The producer had taken a party of the actual survivors back for a reunion, at the invitation, as she believed, of the East German government. So that, when the moment for departure came and she was presented with an enormous bill, she panicked. Fearing that they would all be incarcerated once again, she wrote a personal cheque, then cancelled it as soon as her party was safely back in the West. Long negotiations between the East German authorities and the BBC had ensued. In the end the BBC had admitted liability and paid up. Or so the BBC claimed. The East Germans, however, claimed that they had never received the money.

Establishing this much of the story was a triumph in itself. What Dennis went on to discover, though, was that, while the BBC had indeed paid the money into an East Berlin bank, the bank had put it into the wrong account, where it had been sitting unnoticed ever since. He had not only saved our film, but had released the BBC from the spell that had so long and so mysteriously blocked all their news coverage of the German Democratic Republic.

The finished film was a success, too, so we decided to follow it up by proposing another about the other great German-speaking capital, Vienna. This was an even more triumphant demonstration of Dennis's powers, because he got it commissioned not just by one department of the BBC but two simultaneously. He may have thought – rightly, as it turned out – that this would give us the possibility of playing one off against the other. Perhaps it was simply a demonstration of virtuosity for its own sake, since this time he took me with him to see him in action. First with Bill Morton, in Light Entertainment, who was famous for his popular touch, and who told us that what he expected was a light-hearted travelogue featuring the Big Wheel in the Prater, the Lipizzaner horses and a lot of Johann Strauss waltzes. Dennis let him know how pleased we were to have this sorted out for us, and we moved on to John Drummond, in Music and Arts, a committed cardinal of high culture, who told us that he expected the film to focus on Schoenberg and the development of atonalism. Dennis thanked him no less warmly. What I can't remember now is how either of them reacted when the finished film turned out to be about Klimt, Schiele and the other artists of the Secession, together with the music of neither Strauss nor Schoenberg but exclusively Mahler.

Mahler was a belated discovery in life for me, and one of the joys of our Vienna collaboration. Out of all the many things Dennis knew about – or quickly found out about for the project in hand – music was his real speciality. He went on later in his career to set up vast international co-productions of operas and oratorios that won him major international prizes, and led eventually to his becoming head of the BBC's music programming. His only practical skill in music was a mastery of the gramophone and the tape recorder, together with the film-editing and track-laying tables. I don't think I ever heard him so much as hum or whistle to himself – and I was astonished, many years later, by an old recording of him performing at a Music and Arts Christmas party. He was singing – and singing strong and true, with real feeling – a version he had written for himself of Tevye the Milkman's song from *Fiddler on the Roof*, 'If I Were a Rich Man'. If he were a rich man, he sang, he would be able to make the programmes he wanted to make without having have to go out and hustle for international co-production money. Perhaps it wasn't such a bad thing that he hadn't been a rich man, I've sometimes felt since, or the world would have missed out on a lot of virtuoso pitching.

Meanwhile, in parallel with his rise through the television arts establishment, we went on with our occasional collaborations. The first was my suggestion. Not a foreign city this time, but London. Or rather, its suburbs, where Dennis and I had both grown up, he in Harrow, in North-West London, I in Ewell, in the south. Much explored already, of course, the suburbs, but almost always in a mocking or patronising way. What I wanted to do was take them seriously for once, as seriously as we had Berlin and Vienna, and to reveal, just as we had with the two cities, why and how they had become what they are.

Our fourth film together, a contribution to the BBC's *Great Railway Journeys* series, took us to the other side of the world, for the four-day journey of the Indian Pacific across Australia, from Sydney to Perth, breaking off halfway for a side trip on an even slower train, the Ghan, named for the Afghan labourers and their camels who had built the line, to Alice Springs, in the very centre of the continent. We had a few adventures on the way. There was a lot of shooting from helicopters, together with journeys across the bush that could only be made in light aircraft. Dennis had discovered, rather suddenly and embarrassingly, while we were doing the helicopter work for the suburbs, that he suffered from airsickness, and the flights in Australia were a torment for him. Events provided some objective justification for his feelings. A day or two after we had finished with our helicopter it was forced to make a crash landing. Then, in a small plane somewhere high over the centre of nowhere, with Dennis already in a bad way, there was a loud explosion and the world around us suddenly changed. The explosion, it became apparent when we were able to think again, was the sound of the canopy violently parting company from the rest of the plane and disappearing into the MacDonnell Ranges beneath us. The change in the world around us was the air now blasting our faces and howling round our ears at 130 miles an hour.

I think it was in the same plane that we later had another little problem. The remote airstrip in the middle of the bush where we were planning to land turned out to be occupied already – by brumbies, wild horses, grazing on a patch of grass growing there.

'No worries,' said our pilot with wonderful Australian insouciance. 'We'll just chase them off.' We left our stomachs where they were, a thousand feet or so up in the air, and fell out of the sky at them like a dive-bomber. The brumbies, almost as alarmed as Dennis, fled into the bush. That particular patch of grass was evidently irresistible, though, and by the time we'd circled round to line up with the runway again they were back. Five times we dived at them; five times Dennis died; five times the brumbies fled; five times they came back. And we really needed that runway. The tank was almost empty. We had brought the fuel for the trip back to the next nearest landing site, the aerodrome where we had taken off, but it was in jerry-cans in our luggage compartment, and couldn't be transferred to the tank until we were on the ground. 'No worries,' said our pilot, with perhaps just a little less insouciance than before. 'We'll find a smooth bit in the bush somewhere.' He flew as low as he dared while he tried to make out a stretch of ground beneath us free of rocks, ant-hills, rabbit-warrens or dead kangaroos. By the time we were back on the earth and no longer bouncing, my feelings about flying in small planes were rather similar to Dennis's.

Then, as a *quid pro quo* for the suburbs, we made a film about a subject that Dennis had long had his eye on: Jerusalem. Nine years went by before our next film together, about Prague, and by this time Dennis had not only won prizes for his big international music productions, but had moved up through the jungle of Music and Arts to become head of music programming. At some cost to his character, I discovered. The obverse of Dennis's talent for charming people had always been an almost equal capacity for being rude to them; as he focussed on someone he was interested in impressing he sometimes quite literally turned his back on anyone else who happened to be present. By the time we came to make the Prague film, the strains of office politics, possibly exacerbated by his having given up smoking, had led him not only to ignore people but to pick on them and bully them. The target here was our very hard-working and efficient local associate producer, Michael Havas. I found this perhaps harder to bear than Michael himself did, and I was driven to remonstrate with Dennis. He agreed to apologise to Michael – but almost immediately went back to treating him as some kind of delinquent and backward servant. This culminated in an explosion of rage at the airport as we left that cast a retrospective pall over the entire shoot, when he discovered that Michael had let our rushes go through the X-ray machine. They had all been processed already, so it was difficult to know how they could be affected by X-rays, but Dennis subjected Michael to a public dressing-down for his supposed ignorance and incompetence that could be heard over the entire airport.

I seem to recall that it was in the middle of the Prague shoot that he flew back to London to do the crucial interview that took him out of the world in which he had spent his entire professional life so far. His natural next step upwards at Music and Arts, to be overall head of the department, had been frustrated by the rise of his great rival, Alan Yentob. So he left the BBC and became general director of English National Opera.

I suppose running ENO was the pinnacle of his career. He certainly looked the part. The bushy beard had become neatly trimmed. The bouncing largeness of the young trainee had modulated into the imposing largeness of the public figure. The taste for subverting authority had been overtaken by the ability to exercise it. His first marriage, like mine, had broken up, and he had married

Sally Groves, daughter of the conductor Charles Groves and herself a music publisher – the perfect partner, who knew everyone in the world of music and was loved by them all. To see them receiving their guests together at the Coliseum on the first night of a new production was to see the king and queen, she as gracious and human as he was majestic. I suspect, from our experiences in Prague and later, that her charm was quite often needed.

Now our collaboration took a new turn: an opera. Or at any rate an operetta. The founding principle of ENO was, and is, to sing in English, and Dennis asked me to translate Offenbach's *La belle Hélène* for them. I had never seen or heard the piece, and I had never before attempted any kind of libretto. Claire and I had finally got married, though, and as we drove around south-western France on our honeymoon we played the recording Dennis had sent me of the French original. I was won over by the sheer sparkling freshness of the music.

The book, though, was another matter, even though it was by Meilhac and Halévy, who wrote many successful librettos for Offenbach, and who later provided Bizet with the book for *Carmen*. For a start it followed the depressing convention of the French *opéra comique* (as *Carmen* also does) of interspersing the songs with leaden prose scenes. A lot of the plot was pretty much incomprehensible unless you knew more about Greek mythology than any modern audience was likely to, and the facetiousness with which it was treated had long lost the power to shock. The lyrics were crisp – but they were going to be lost in translation anyway. So I said I would do it only if I could provide my own story and characters, and move it from mythical Greece to where it seemed naturally at home – the get-rich-quick world of Second Empire Paris in which it had first been produced, and which had rather a lot in common with post-Thatcherite Britain. Dennis allowed himself to be persuaded.

He provided me with the perfect collaborator – James Holmes, who would also conduct. I've just re-read our correspondence over the next few months, and was shaken by the sheer amount of labour that I put into the enterprise, and that Jim put into helping me make my text singable and musically literate. When we thought we had finished – though we hadn't, not by any means – Jim undertook the most monstrous labour of all: accompanying himself on the piano as he sang the entire text through to Dennis single-handed. Dennis, I couldn't help noticing, only too characteristically failed to thank Jim for this extraordinary feat. Or to say anything to him at all, even to offer him a cup of tea.

Still, he gave us the green light, and we began to set up a rather sumptuous production, with Ian Judge directing and the ENO's biggest star, Lesley Garrett, singing the lead. As if we didn't have our hands full enough with this, Dennis agreed to make another film with me at the same time. The subject this time was Budapest, and the proposal came from an independent producer, Paul Neuberg, who had been born and brought up there. Dennis took a lot of persuading, in view of his commitments at ENO, and I don't know whether his finally agreeing was a tribute to the powers of another skilled persuader, or whether he simply couldn't bear to let me do a collaboration with someone else.

So he was once again the director – but this time not the producer. And at the same time producer, but not director, of the opera. His shifts back and forth between the two roles were spectacular. I would come into breakfast at our hotel in Budapest and find him festooned in the long trails of tractor-fed fax paper that electronic

communication involved at the time, already an hour or two into
ENO business. 'If I can't get it into Ian's head that he's got to get the
cost of the set down,' Dennis producer would snarl, 'I'm cancelling
the production.' Then Paul, the producer of our film, would arrive,
and Dennis would move into director mode. 'What do you mean,'
he would snarl, 'I've got to get the costs of equipment hire down?'
The pressures of his new job – and doing a second job at the same
time – were perhaps telling on him, in spite of his having taken up
smoking again, and this time it was Paul who became the target.
Dennis was so rude to him, even before we had actually started
filming, that I threatened to walk off the location. Not that my
anger had any more effect than my polite remonstrations in Prague.

All the same, those two simultaneous productions of ours, the
opera and the film, were the apotheosis of our long collaboration.
Or should have been. The film went down all right, so far as I
recall, but the opera (finally entitled, after much argument, *La belle
Vivette*) didn't. Ian Judge's production was spectacular and Lesley
Garrett charmed the audiences as she always did. The first night
seemed to go as well as any of my first nights ever had, and the
sheer volume of applause that I was pushed on stage to face from
that huge house at the end was like nothing I had ever known. But
the reviews next morning were dismissive; the critics thought that I
shouldn't have messed around with a piece that had proved itself so
thoroughly in so many earlier productions. In any case there was a
structural problem for any new text at the Coliseum. The acoustics
of that vast barn were notoriously difficult – but it was an item
of faith with the management in those days not to use surtitles,
which might have seemed to undercut ENO's whole *raison d'être* of
singing in English. So I don't think the audience caught many of

the words over which Jim and I had laboured so long and hard. It was the production and the music that the first-night audience had been cheering.

Vivette wasn't the only thing that went wrong for Dennis at ENO, and less than two years later he phoned me to say that he was leaving the job. At once, that day, without notice. Resigning? Fired? He wouldn't say, or explain in any way what had happened. I think it was probably a fundamental difference of opinion with the Board about the building. The severe problems of the Coliseum were not restricted to the acoustics. There was very little space back-stage – not enough to accommodate the sets of all the shows in the repertory that were currently not playing, and which therefore had to be stored in trucks on the street at the back. Conditions for the artists were very poor, and I believe the basement and the sewerage had become rather disgustingly confused. Dennis, I know, wanted to build a new theatre away from the West End; the Board, on the other hand, thought that the problems were outweighed by the old theatre's familiar and accessible location at the heart of the entertainment district. Feelings on both sides ran high, and I suspect that the difference of opinion was exacerbated by the abrasive style of professional relations that Dennis had come to adopt over the years. I only hope that his generosity and boldness in giving me such a free hand with the Offenbach hadn't added to his difficulties.

He was still not quite fifty, and his departure from ENO was the end of his career as an administrator. I suppose his refusal to talk about it may have been a condition of whatever understanding he had come to with the Board. If so, he honoured it very thoroughly, and I never discovered, then or later, what he really felt about this huge caesura in his life. I think, I hope, that he felt at any rate some element of liberation. He and Sally were certainly able to spend more time at the house they had acquired in the south of Italy. He took the opportunity to write a book about an author whose work we had come across when we were making the Vienna film together, Joseph Roth; his masterpiece, *The Radetzky March*, and another of his novels, *The Emperor's Tomb*, are about the Central Europe of the Austro-Hungarian Empire whose last years we had both become so fascinated by. He also made some more presented documentaries – not for TV this time but for radio – and not only as producer/director but also taking my role as writer/presenter. He went to look for his family's origins, somewhere in the Russian Pale of Settlement, and turned out to be a natural presenter – better, I think, than I had ever been. Whether he had as much fun on his own as we usually had together I don't know, nor whether he ever got as impatient with himself as he had with some of his associates.

I got the impression, though, that he didn't find life as a freelance entirely easy. Sally said that he was sometimes very depressed, and I think he abandoned another book. Then things seemed to be looking up. He had a lot of plans for the house in Puglia, and according to Sally some rather attractive professional prospects. But in 2015, only seven years after he had left ENO, he was diagnosed with leukaemia. That was in January. A month later he and Sally came to lunch, and afterwards we set off on our travels together again. Only a little stroll down the road this time, but after half a mile he was so overcome by exhaustion that he couldn't even manage the half-mile home. That short walk turned out to be the last journey we were ever to make together, because in the next few weeks another cancer was discovered, and by the beginning of April he was dead.

He had a traditional Jewish funeral, for which, movingly, his son learned enough Hebrew from scratch to say the Kaddish. Then in the autumn his old colleagues in the BBC organised a memorial, and produced it with a professionalism that was worthy of him and the trade he had followed with such distinction. He had been loved by many people, in spite of his dictatorial moments. And, right at the end, after we had all offered our tributes, and all laughed and all felt sad, they sprang that last surprise – Dennis himself, singing to us, like Tevye the Milkman, about how things might have been if they hadn't been the way they were.

Play Mate

Biarritz in summer, and in fine weather the view from the top of the cliff above the Côte des Basques is like some vast and glorious stage set. Out over the wild Bay of Biscay to the distant blue mountains of northern Spain, and immediately beneath you one of the most famous beaches in Europe – miles and miles of sand stretching south into the eye of the sun towards Saint-Jean-de-Luz. From somewhere far beyond the horizon the great blue Atlantic rollers move patiently towards their landfall in France, then splinter into shifting lines of white surf, with a straggling flotsam of suntanned young bodies balancing their wildly manoeuvring boards. In among them, any summer's day in the last fifty or so years, you might sometimes have been just able to make out one tiny but important additional detail: a single body-surfer, a discreet and stately human torpedo buried in the tumbling white chaos, arms outstretched in front of him in salutation to the sun god, head lifting nobly clear of the water every now and then for a mouthful of air. It would have been Michael Blakemore, a local resident for as often as he could manage it, possibly the world's last remaining body-surfer, and certainly one of its greatest theatre directors.

Michael and I were friends for fifty years, and for forty of them professional colleagues. I wasn't the only playwright he worked with and he wasn't the only director who did my plays. But we did do ten original productions together, and another eight revivals and overseas follow-ups. Very occasionally there would be another body buried in the surf not far away from his, struggling to learn the knack of catching a wave, and it would be me, taking a break from our work on some new enterprise.

He chose Biarritz and its surf because it was Europe's closest equivalent to the beaches of Australia, where he grew up. His early life he has described in his two volumes of memoirs, and better than anybody else is likely to. The first takes him through his childhood in Sydney and his arrival as a young man in a still grey and tired post-war Britain to start his career. It's entitled *Arguments With England*, but he had had plenty of arguments with Australia, too, before he left, principally directed against his father, a successful Sydney doctor, and the hearty sporting culture of Australia at the time. He not only wrote about his childhood – he made a film about it, *A Personal History of the Australian Surf*, and in it, cunningly and touchingly, he plays not himself but his father, who is finally forced to concede his son some grudging respect because the swimming and surfing that he loves will just about pass as manly sports, and because he is skilled enough at them to become a member of the socially elite local Surf Lifesaving Club.

He started his life in England as an actor, and the memoirs follow him through the provincial reps and seedy touring digs of the time to joining the Royal Shakespeare Company at Stratford-upon-Avon (whose complex internal politics are the background of his one novel, *Next Season*), and then to becoming artistic director of the Glasgow Citizens' Theatre. It was here that he had his first real triumph – directing the original production of Peter Nichols's *A Day in the Death of Joe Egg*, which launched the careers of both author and director.

This was in 1967, and the second volume of his memoirs, *Stage Blood*, takes him on to join the National Theatre, then in its own early days under the direction of Laurence Olivier. It was about this time that we first met, because my then wife Gill and I had become friends with the Nicholses, and Michael was directing Peter's next play, *The National Health*. But the book finishes before he and I began our long working partnership. So here, briefly, is my own account of it, as I remember it.

• • •

Michael was not the first director with whom I did more than one show. Christopher Morahan directed two of my Chekhov translations, and a film, *Clockwise*. Most of my own early plays were produced by Michael Codron, and by the time we had got to the third, *Alphabetical Order*, he had teamed me up with another Michael, Michael Rudman, who was then running the Hampstead Theatre. You can see a picture of us in a *Sunday Times* feature on writer–director pairs, Rudman standing rather grandly behind my chair, very handsome and man-of-the-world, me sitting like a sub-missive bride. There was some truth in the appearance. He was a Texan, and he had the alpha-male wisecracking American style that made everyone around him, me included, his straight man. I mostly enjoyed the role, but always felt slightly wrong-footed and provincial.

By the time we came to my fourth play, though, *Make and Break*, Michael Rudman had moved to the National Theatre, and I urged Michael Codron to offer it to Michael Blakemore. (Difficult to tell this story without confusion when all four of the people involved were on first-name terms – and all our first names are Michael. Not

179

a problem that I should have allowed to arise, of course, if we had been characters I had invented. To keep things clear among ourselves, when we referred to each other we took to adding an initial: Michael C., Michael B., Michael F.)

Michael C. was curiously resistant to the idea of Michael B. He admitted his talents. 'But would he make me laugh?' he said. I think the problem was not really to do with Michael B.'s sense of humour or supply of theatrical gossip – it was that they had in fact done a production together in the past, David Hare's *Knuckle*, and there had been difficulties of some sort. In the event, once Michael C. had conceded, Michael B. kept him reasonably well amused for the next forty years.

As he did me. I have got on with almost all the directors that I have worked closely with. But my relationship with Michael B. became part of my life, and we were always completely at ease together. I enjoyed his affectionate Australian joshing, which reached its apogee when he served as best man at my wedding to Claire in 1991, and made an outrageously funny speech that completely upstaged the bridegroom's own efforts. I even appreciated most of his rather wide range of foibles. He was interested in everything, and well informed and articulate about it all. He talked readily about the many personal complications in his life, in the way that men are said to avoid. I may even have said a word or two about some of the ones in mine. Something I didn't do with all the friends I have written about here, or with some of the others I haven't. So which of them was my closest friend? I don't know! It's not a beauty competition! Little girls may have to have a really, really best friend (who suddenly and painfully is no longer even a worst friend). But you can have different sorts of friend. What's so nice about some of them is that you talk to them about your most private feelings. What's so nice about others is that you never do. Then again, with some friends it's a joy to have some common enterprise to work on. With others you couldn't so much as put up a tent together without irritating each other.

. . .

The more I worked on plays with Michael the less I understood how he did it. To help actors find inside themselves the characters suggested by the dialogue that the playwright has set down, and to bring their interactions into three-dimensional physical reality, is an elusive skill. It's hard enough doing plays that have been done before – and Michael did notable versions of Chekhov and O'Neill, of Coward and Travers. But at least with a classic or the revival of an old success you know that the play itself works. That's why it's being done again. But with a new play you can never know until you actually get it in front of the public. The possibility of failure and humiliation haunts the enterprise, and you have to keep your eyes closed to it, like the climber or the tightrope walker never looking down into the depths they can feel reaching up to swallow them.

A new play, a play that has never been performed before – this is the real test of a director. You have to understand the possibilities of what's on the page in front of you, which is often by no means obvious when no one's ever understood it before – often not even the writer. You have to be selfless enough to work with the writer's intentions, and not adjust them to your own. You also have to have the judgement to see where the author has gone wrong, or not understood the full implications of what he is trying to do, and the confidence and skill to help him get it right. And then, at the end of it all, to accept as the real accolade for your work the author's getting most of any credit going.

This is where Michael's greatest mastery has always lain, in the first productions of new plays. Never more so than in the case of our biggest success together, *Noises Off.* It's difficult now to recollect how discouraging the text of this looked when I first sent it to Michael C. and Michael B. Act One is mostly a pastiche of a wretched sex farce, Act Two a tangle of interlocking stage directions, while Act Three in this early version turned halfway through into a serious disquisition on (so far as I recall) order and disorder. Sorting all this out must have been the most searching test ever of Michael's skills.

We do our work together on the text in Biarritz. Michael's house there is the great constant of his life, that outlives four different London addresses and two marriages. I stayed there several times over the years, sometimes with my family, sometimes for work, sometimes for pleasure. It isn't what you might expect a holiday home to be like – it's a serious nineteenth-century house near the centre of town, tall and narrow, where you can slip out to the baker's across the road in the morning for croissants, and go just a bit further down the road to the market for freshly caught sardines. Or round the corner for that clifftop view of the Bay of Biscay, and the path zigzagging down through the tamarisk bushes to that irresistible surf.

But Biarritz for Michael isn't just Bondi plus croissants; over the years he becomes deeply absorbed in the life and history of the town, and of the whole Basque region. The rooms are full of French railway posters from the town's heyday in the belle époque, and comfortably worn furniture and artefacts from the local *brocanteries*. And, on evenings when he is not treating his guests to endless films of one more or less identical surfie after another riding more or less identical waves, he is telling them about the oddity of the Basque language, which has no known connections with any other language or language group in the world, or taking them out to watch pelota, the local sport.

In September every year, when the weather in Biarritz is most likely to be crystalline and the surf most elegantly sculpted by wind and current, there is always a total absence of Michael from London and the theatre world. September is sacrosanct; September is Biarritz. Which is why, on 6 September 1981, with autumn production deadlines upon us but the year's best surf waiting, I am arriving there to start our collaboration on the enterprise that will change the next forty years of life for both of us.

The way we work is always the same. I read my text aloud to him, and, since I have no acting ability, do it so badly that I lose all confidence in it. Michael listens expressionlessly, not smiling, certainly not laughing, but absorbed, seeing it happening inside his head, and thinking how it could happen better. On I plough, till Michael stops me, perhaps to think for a moment and then continue, or to ask a stupid question, or to make a stupid suggestion. I struggle to conceal my impatience and irritation . . . then slowly begin to see the shrewdness of the question, the possibilities opened up by the suggestion . . .

In those blue September days in Biarritz he suggests quite a lot of the farcical business that I will eventually get the credit for. The most demanding test of his powers, though, is the beginning of Act

Two. In my text the curtain rises to reveal that we are backstage at the Theatre Royal, Ashton-under-Lyne. Upstage, simultaneously, the Theatre Royal's own curtain rises on the show we are seeing from behind. The simultaneity is an elegant notion, it seems to me, and I am deeply wedded to it. 'Yes,' says Michael patiently, 'but no one's going to have the slightest idea where we are, or what's going on. There's got to be a scene before the play-within-the-play begins where we explain everything. And where we also make clear what the relations between the characters now are – who's pursuing whom, who's fallen out with whom, who misunderstands what.'

At some point, as we argue about all this, Michael's eye begins to wander to the blue sky outside the window. Something tells him that the unseen surf is coming to perfection as the tide changes, and work is abandoned. We're off, down the zigzag path. After lunch, while Michael is relaxing with the newspaper, I draft the new scene. In fact, whether through the tonic effect of the surf or the fundamental soundness of Michael's ideas, it practically writes itself. By the time Michael has finished the paper I have it ready for him – and it's the best scene in the play.

• • •

Imagining those unforthcoming marks on paper into a world in real space and real time is the director's first task. The next is turning the disembodied characters who inhabit it into real flesh-and-blood human beings. Casting: it looks obvious with hindsight, when it's been done well, but the leap from notion to physical reality is always hard. In your memory you have recollections of an indefinite range of particular actors with particular personalities. You've seen them playing an indefinite range of particular characters in other plays. They did them well, of course they did, or you wouldn't be considering them. But the more fully they were those other characters, the harder it is to imagine them being the hopefully rather different characters in your own play. And when you have at last managed to identify the one real person in the world who might become your still non-existent one . . . they've just accepted something else, don't like the part you're offering, want too much money, won't sign for long enough for the producer to cover his costs, are waiting for a film or a television series. You have to expunge their face from the picture you have formed of your character, and start imagining all over again. And you know that, if you get the answer wrong, you're never going to make the play come to life.

We do this part of the work not under the open blue skies of Gascony, but in the blue fug of Michael C.'s cigar smoke in his office high up above Regent Street. Or rather Michaels B. and C. do it, while I sit observing their shrewd professional interchanges like a spectator at a tennis match. And even when we are done, and Michael B. has the whole thing secure inside his head and our nine real people contracted and waiting, that haunting, debilitating uncertainty remains. 'I will do my best with it,' says Michael seriously, as we set off for the first rehearsal. 'But I simply do not know whether it will work or not.' This is not what he tells the actors when we all sit round a table to read the play through. Instead he gives them, as he always does, an account of the play and its background that is so well thought out, so coherent and so compelling, that I, at any rate, am completely persuaded.

What happens in the rehearsal room thereafter I don't really know. After that first day I stay away. Some writers like to be there throughout, making suggestions and rewriting. But Michael and I have already done everything we can do together for the moment. We both feel that it's a bit confusing for the actors to have an alternative authority present with a possibly alternative response to what they're doing. Then again, things develop so slowly from day to day in rehearsals that it's difficult for everyone to see where they've got to and where they're going. It can sometimes be helpful to have the writer come in when there's actually some finished piece of work to look at – the run of an act, say – and to see where things have got to.

Sometimes, when I arrive, they're not ready to begin the promised run, so I do see a little of Michael at work. Doing nothing, apparently. Except being patient and courteous, and keeping everyone involved and entertained. When we do get to the run, everyone is a little on edge because the writer is in, and it's difficult not to see him as the visiting magistrate, the inspector general, the authority on the text, who is going to complain and condemn. He's not, of course. He's going to be amazed and grateful because, once again, the magic has begun to happen. That apparent doing-nothing of Michael's, that patience and courtesy, have somehow transmuted the base metal of the script into a substance that has flecks of gold in it. It's true that I have been making notes, and I have a list of thirty-seven small ungrateful carping comments that it will take all Michael's practised patience to listen to. But once again he has pretty much done it; he has taken those unforthcoming marks of mine on the paper of the text, those permutations of the twenty-six dully familiar hieroglyphs, and turned them into living people with blood in their veins and feelings in their hearts – people who are involved in an event that is happening in front of our eyes in three dimensions and in time. Into something remarkably like life itself – only better organised and more comprehensible, because life has not had the benefit of being directed by Michael.

• • •

And then the previews begin, and we reach the next great challenge to the director's ability: an audience.

However carefully one has prepared, the reaction of an audience almost always comes as a surprise. They don't understand some fundamental point that one has taken such care to make plain. They don't laugh at things that were wonderfully funny until they were watched in such hostile silence. They do laugh at things that everyone has long since forgotten were intended to be funny. Which in my case, with *Noises Off*, is practically everything. We have suddenly got back to something that had vanished beneath all that work in Biarritz and Michael C.'s office and the rehearsal room, like the plants beneath the dull soil of winter, and which has sprung gloriously forth again, like those same plants when spring returns.

Or has for the first two and a half acts. Then, in the middle of Act Three, when the farce makes its sudden swerve into epistemology, we are plunged abruptly back into January. The audience, we discover, does not want a disquisition on the nature of order at this late stage in the evening. Did neither Michael nor I foresee this in Biarritz? Or – perhaps more likely – did he foresee it and warn me, only for me to dig my heels in? So, more rethinking and rewriting – and no blue sky outside the window now, no surf waiting at the bottom of the zigzag path. The play has passed into the hands of the actors, who have to learn and rehearse all our changes. So we have to cut it back and invent new material bit by agonising bit from night to night, like surgeons tailoring a series of operations to what the patient can bear at any one time. We continue until the cast revolt and refuse to learn any more versions. Then, during the run itself, every time a new cast takes over, we perform further surgery. A director's work is never done! If it had taken Dr Frankenstein this long to get his monster going . . . he might have ended up with a less monstrous monster.

• • •

Michael has his complications. His apparently glowing good health co-exists with a susceptibility to all kinds of illness. An endless series of skin cancers, caused presumably by all that Bondi and Biarritz sunlight. A fistula that has made sitting through rehearsals of one of his early productions a torment before it's dealt with. An irregular heartbeat, corrected by a pacemaker that causes more trouble itself. A replacement knee, and problems with it. He can't see very well out of one of his eyes, hit by a frisbee on an Australian beach when he was a boy, and late in life he goes blind in it. All these rather dramatic problems are played out on a background of common colds and influenzas that go on for weeks, and various unspecified forms of malaise that last for even longer. Any enquiry about how he is expects the answer, 'Terrible.' It's difficult to know exactly where objectively diagnosable illness shades into hypochondria. Things would no doubt be even worse if he hadn't discovered an ever-changing series of miracle cures and prophylactics – vitamin supplements, extracts from exotic fruits and roots. I arrive at his door to work on one of our productions with a cold, and he refuses to let me over the threshold until I have eaten a large clove of raw garlic. For a time his house is guarded by a machine that blows out negative ions, because negative ions have a positive effect upon the negative influence of the positive ions that surround us.

He has a pessimistic fascination with the world's concealed environmental hazards, and likewise with all the criminal conspiracies that are going on behind the scenes of government and big business. He is often beset by suspicions, sometimes not entirely unjustified, particularly in New York, that the producers he is working for are up to something nefarious behind his back. He weaves all this into an attractively comic performance of himself, which includes hostility to an arbitrary selection of modern technology. He never learns to drive, and, when I chauffeur him, he mocks my inability to find parking places in central London immediately outside where he wants to go. He has an aversion to the London Underground and the New York subway, and prefers to risk missing trains and planes by sitting out traffic jams in taxis and hire cars. His faith in machines that blow out negative ions goes with a rather less rational and more socially obstructive refusal to use email.

Biarritz and ginseng root are not his only joys. He loves old Hollywood movies, particularly the kind that cineastes later call *noirs*. The passion that surprises me most is for Brahms. He may just possibly have learned this from his father, in spite of all their differences; there is a wonderful sequence in *A Personal History* of his father driving him to the beach, with the Sydney Heads in the background, and obsessively whistling the same meaningless musical phrase over and over again – until, in the film, it dissolves into the full orchestral version of what Michael discovered only many years later was the big cantabile theme in the last movement of Brahms's first symphony.

I, too, have intense feelings about the music of Brahms, so perhaps it's one of the bonds between us. An unconscious one, if so, because for Michael it was so private that I only found out that we shared it after we had worked together for forty years.

• • •

One of his arguments with Australia in his memoirs is the inaccessibility, while he was growing up, both of the girls of his own age who he felt should have been ready to be seduced by him and of the older women who should have been seducing him. He makes up handsomely for this early sexual deprivation later. Women, it turns out once he has reached England, find him as attractive as he does them. Rather more of them, in fact, over the years, than he can manage without problems and anguish.

When we first begin working together he is still with his first wife, Shirley, whose bright good nature apparently allows him a fair amount of latitude – even another long-term relationship around which he collects a separate circle of friends. I am one of the Shirley circle, and I never meet the alternative partner – never even hear Michael mention her name until long after the arrangement has finished and she has graduated to being simply yet another of his enduring problems. Then, while he is working in Australia, he begins a third serious relationship, this time with the designer Tanya McCallin. This, after many storms, becomes his second marriage, and my friendship with Michael expands to become a friendship between the two couples, Michael and Tanya, and me and my own second wife, Claire.

We love both Tanya's stage designs and her open friendliness. She does a brilliant set for a play Claire has written, and takes her shopping for clothes. It's a good period for all four of us. We are in and out of each other's houses, and travels, and lives, and we love their two daughters. We never quite get over our distress when the marriage somehow sours. Another serious affair may have been among the causes, or the result, or both. They separate but never divorce, and the tangled bond of festering recriminations and lingering regrets is never quite severed, though it's succeeded by yet another relationship that begins when Michael is working in New York, and continues across those 3,500 daunting miles of cold North Atlantic.

And in some ways, in spite of all the friends and attachments, all the adventures and their aftermath, he remains notably self-contained, and content with his own company. A lot of his working life is spent living in hotel rooms in New York or Sydney or elsewhere, and he seems on the whole happy to pad about in a dressing gown, with room service and the television news, and a pool somewhere on the premises. After his second marriage breaks up, his home life settles into something more like his travelling mode – long days on his own in a comfortable mansion flat that looks out over the rooftops of Bloomsbury, sitting far into the night watching the developing dramas and scandals of American political life on CNN.

He has his professional disappointments as well as his successes. I don't think he ever really regrets not succeeding Olivier as head of the National Theatre, as Olivier himself seems to have wanted. But he spends literally years declining other projects as he waits for a big New York musical, based on Daphne du Maurier's *Rebecca*, that is always just about to happen and notoriously never quite does. He remains doggedly loyal to another musical that he does direct in New York, *The Life*, and devotes enormous efforts to bringing it to London, where it flares brilliantly but briefly in a fringe theatre, never to be seen again. He longs to move into films. When we have a reasonable success in the West End with my translation of *Uncle Vanya*, I write a screenplay from it for him. It's still there somewhere in the files, waiting like so many of the world's screenplays for that fearful and glorious day that will surely come, when the files will open and give up their dead, and in the twinkling of an eye find producers, stars, studios and the immortality that films are the only dramatic form to offer.

It's *Vanya* that leads to the only feature film that Michael ever does manage to set up, apart from a version of another Peter Nichols play, *Privates on Parade*, that he has made a success on stage. Not with my screenplay but with one he writes himself, that shifts the story from Russia to the Australian outback, under the title *Country Life*. I'm sometimes surprised, when I think about it, that directing it didn't finish him. It's shot in a New South Wales heatwave, with the smoke of bush fires all around the location, and Michael not only directing it but playing the dried-up and disappointed Professor Serebryakov in a three-piece tweed suit. And in a performance that, like his speech at my wedding, rather upstages his own stars.

• • •

By no means all the eighteen productions that we do together are hits; sometimes that haunting uncertainty turns out to be justified. He manages to stay clear of my biggest flop, *Look Look*, about a theatre audience – loyally offering to do it if I really want him to, but telling me plainly that he doesn't think it will work. So Michael Codron and I defiantly go ahead with another director, and Michael B. turns out to have been rather spectacularly right. Our evening of one-acters, *Alarms and Excursions*, does reasonably well in the West End, but doesn't go to New York. *Make and Break* and *Democracy* are solid successes in London and do go to America, but don't quite make it there. (It was probably Leonard Rossiter's performance as Garrard, the single-minded businessman in *Make and Break*, that carried the play in London, and one of Michael's enduring regrets is that he cast American actors in *Democracy* to play the German chancellor Willy Brandt, and the spy Günther Guillaume who brought him down, instead of the unsurpassable leads from the London production, Roger Allam and Conleth Hill.) Two of our productions together, *Here* and *Afterlife*, are failures even in London. I find both especially painful experiences – in the case of *Here*, about a young couple setting up their life together, because it has always been perhaps my favourite among my own plays, and with *Afterlife*, about the great Austrian producer-director Max Reinhardt, because Michael is eighty years old at the time, and it will almost certainly be our last production together, our swansong; and also because I see in its depiction of Reinhardt, (Roger Allam once again, and once again unsurpassable) some kind of oblique tribute to both Michael Blakemore as a director and Michael Codron as a producer.

But we have a success in both London and New York with

Benefactors, about a public housing scheme and its architects, and our two really big hits, *Noises Off* and *Copenhagen*. The text of *Copenhagen* must look almost as unpromising as the earlier play did when Michael first reads it – not, this time, too many stage directions, but none at all. He has the courage to respect its austerity, and to stage it with nothing but the three actors and three chairs. To this apparently simple picture he adds just the most sparing touches of theatrical colour: the watching eyes of the audience on all sides of the action, a sound to echo the Bohrs' recurring memories of the day their eldest son drowned, and another to make suddenly and terrifyingly real the nuclear bomb that the Germans never actually built. He directs the productions not only in London and New York but in Sydney and Paris – and, on a memorable evening in New York, becomes the first director ever to win two Tony awards in the same year, one for *Copenhagen*, and one for his dazzling revival of *Kiss Me, Kate*.

• • •

I love joining him on his travels. But I get the best of it. He has spent all those long days shut up in some windowless rehearsal room, all those long evenings in that lonely hotel room. Then, when he's got everything pretty much ready, I arrive for the start of previews, or the first night, or both. If it's New York, it's usually evening for him, but for me, straight off the plane, somewhere in the small hours. We go out for dinner together in some modest local restaurant he knows, he pleased to see a familiar face from the life he left behind, me high on jetlag and anticipation in this unreal sudden new world of bright lights and yellow cabs, as I listen to him telling me which members of the cast are going to be particularly good, which still haven't learned their lines, and what secret mischief he suspects the producers are up to.

I recall a day of dreamlike happiness in Washington, DC. This is during the run of *Noises Off* at the Kennedy Center, where we have been putting in yet more rewrites before the big opening on Broadway. We are going to watch the latest improvement to Act Three at the midweek matinee, but neither of us can bear to sit through the first two acts yet again. We walk round and round the roof terrace of the theatre on our own. It's that beautiful blue and gold fall weather that you get in America, with the heat of summer long gone and the cold of winter still unimaginable. The pale sky is full of little white balls of cloud that seem to have a characteristically American chic. We walk and talk, absolutely at ease together. What do we talk so easily about? I have no recollection. Not the show. We have done our best with it for now, and we have to leave it to its own devices. Our feelings, perhaps, and all the other things that men don't talk about.

Michael seems to get a particular pleasure from doing *Copenhagen* in Paris. He has been summoned urgently to take over a production that is already in rehearsal, after the original director has got it into a hopeless tangle and lost the confidence of the cast. Not an easy situation, particularly since he is working in a language of which he knows scarcely a single word, unbelievably, even after all his years in Biarritz (though he has, it's true, done productions before in Danish and Hebrew, languages of which he knows even less). He spends his free time exploring the city instead of sitting in his hotel, as he does in New York, and the producer he is working for is a former star of the French theatre with a wealthy husband who is not entirely unaware of Michael's attractiveness. She is certainly very liberal, he tells me, with oysters and dinners at the Dôme. Michael sweeps away the complicated series of gauzes that the original director has been flying in and out to indicate the various different points in time at which the action occurs, and earns the respect of his notoriously difficult Heisenberg, who was the protagonist in getting Michael's predecessor removed, and who had once assaulted an actress on stage in the middle of a performance. Michael's belated rescue works, and Claire and I join him and Tanya in Paris, once for the premiere and again for Michael and me to collect our subsequent joint Prix Molière. His acceptance speech is in French, to my surprise, though brief and sounding more like a cry from the dock at the Old Bailey: 'Mercy!'

Claire and I also happen to be in Australia while Michael is there to set up the Sydney production of *Copenhagen*, and he takes us back in time for a guided tour of his childhood – north to Palm Beach, where he had his teenage triumph as a lifesaver, south to Bawley Point, where as a boy he and his family had spent the long summer days living in a simple boarding house with neither plumbing nor electricity – then further south still, to the vast horizons of his cousin's sheep farm on the high plains of the Monaro, in the foothills of the Snowy Mountains. He's seventy-three by this time, but that nostalgic excursion to his childhood turns out to be far from valedictory. We still have five more productions of our own to go, and he has other successes to come in both London and New York. He's already eighty-six when he has a hit in both cities with Angela Lansbury in a wonderfully funny and stylish *Blithe Spirit*. In fact, his skill as a director never fades. He's eighty-nine when he at last gets his hard-fought-for London production of *The Life* set up, with a young, largely Black cast who do a show that hurls its colossal verve and energy right into the faces of the audience around the little stage of the Southwark Playhouse.

And then on to our final collaboration and his last show. It's not the triumphant finale with *Afterlife* that we had hoped for eleven years earlier. But in 2019, on the eve of his ninetieth birthday, he starts rehearsing a revival of *Copenhagen* at the Chichester Theatre. Somehow all the old magic works again, and it turns out to be just about as perfect a production as live theatre can ever achieve. Not too bad a note to go out on.

Fire and Ashes

A sweltering night at the end of June 1957, and I'm invited to a late-night party in a Chelsea mews. I'm just down from Cambridge, with all the long preface to my life finally behind me. I have a job starting in September to look forward to and in the meanwhile plans for a last holiday summer of travels and visits with friends, and now, apparently, entry into this stylish world, new to me, of midnight parties in fashionable districts of London. By the time the midsummer sun rises a few hours later, though, all my plans for the next couple of months have vanished like the night itself, and I have been overtaken by the beginnings of a love affair as transforming as the beginnings of the day around me.

I suppose this is really why you go to all those parties when you're young – in the ever-springing hope that you'll meet someone you're going to be in love with, and who's going to be in love with you. Sometimes it had almost happened, or even half-happened; mostly the long hours had gone by in disappointment. And now, suddenly . . .

How exactly it had, though, I can't remember. How we first noticed each other among all the other people with the same hopes packing the little mews garage where the party was held, how we first got talking over the noise of the band and of all the other people struggling to make themselves heard. I can't even remember clearly what she looked like, and until I started writing this I didn't have a photograph of her to remind me, even after everything that followed. A mass of dark hair, a smile, a gentleness of manner. She must have told me her name: Liza. All I remember is that we left the party and walked about the West London streets together for the rest of the night.

It was still hot, and so late that the streets were quiet, most of them so empty you could walk down the middle of them. Which we did, past famous statues and famous shops, through exclusive squares, past the houses of the rich, completely at home in all the elegance and privilege. We must have walked to St James's Park and the streets around Buckingham Palace, because the thing I remember most clearly is the red roadway of Constitution Hill opening in front of us as it was just beginning to get light. And as we walked I suppose we told each other about all the things that people do tell each other about as they fall in love. Our childhoods, our families. The great plans we had for the lives that were opening out in front of us.

She is four years younger than me, and she is at Oxford, at Somerville, where she has just finished her second year reading Greats, otherwise Literae Humaniores, the notoriously demanding four-year-long combination of classics and philosophy that every-one at Oxford is particularly respectful of. I'm not sure whether she had been invited to the party by Veronica Gascoigne, my friend Bamber's sister, who is giving it and is also at Oxford, or by her own brother Nicholas, who is at Cambridge, at Magdalene with Bamber. Our small world! But still, as I have now discovered, with surprises to spring.

There's something a bit old-fashioned about her – something that suggests the expression 'well brought up'. You know she is loving to her family, kindly to strangers in distress, courteous to her tutors. She has been the head girl of her public school, I discover later.

Liza, yes; her name has a straightforwardness that seems exactly right. Particularly when it's combined with the obliquity of her surname: Mrosovsky. Slavonic, certainly – Polish, by the sound of that impossible opening conjunction of consonants, but too unusual, I discover now, to be included in Wikipedia's comprehensive list of Polish surnames.

Liza Mrosovsky. By the time the streets of West London are lit by the risen sun I am completely in love with her. And she, I know, with me. I've been in love with girls before, or thought I was, but it's the first time in the twenty-four years of my life so far that this mutual thunderclap has really happened to me. And I think the first time to her in the twenty years of hers. We have the summer in front of us, and the whole of our lives, and we are in love. I with her, she with me.

We can't bear to part. So here's an original idea for an intimate nightspot to take your new love to: Liverpool Street Station. We go straight there from the streets of West London, sleepless and sleepy, like the two sleepy people in the song. (How, though? By taxi, obviously – but I don't think we either of us have the fare. Is the Tube running already? We can't have walked that far! Can we? Drifted up into the air, perhaps, as in a dream, and floated, side by side.) At Liverpool Street we get the milk train to Cambridge. There I retrieve my dinner jacket and gown from wherever I have left them, collect a fur stole I have hired from an academic outfitters, and after a morning of rehearsals at my college and sunlit green gliding with Liza on the river, walk in procession through the streets to the Senate House, with Liza following through the Saturday shopping crowds on the pavement beside us.

In the Senate House I stand in a group of four, as tradition

203

dictates – each of us holding one of our tutor's fingers like pig-
lets sucking on a sow, or the graduates that we shall so shortly be,
attached to our old university for the rest of our lives – and then we
step up one by one to the vice chancellor on his throne. I kneel and
bow my head, as hot as a haybox in the sweltering June afternoon
under the insulation of my dinner jacket, gown and fur stole. And
as the vice chancellor takes my hand and I wait to hear the magic
Latin incantation that will turn me into a Bachelor of Arts, I feel on
the back of my head the invisible extra benefaction of Liza gazing
down on me from the gallery, and hear – echoing round the entire
Senate House, as it seems to me – the drops of sweat falling one by
one from my forehead on to the black and white tiles of the floor.

When I try to remember the exact details of that extraordinary
couple of days, these are the things that come to mind most sharply:
the red roadway of Constitution Hill in the dawn twilight, and
the sound of my sweat dripping on to the tiled floor of the Senate
House.

• • •

'Dear Michael, *ami de deux nuits-jours*,' begins the letter from her
that arrives a week later, the first of the fifty-six she will write me in
the course of the following six months. It was finding them recently
and reading them again that made me think of trying to circum-
vent, in this one case, the difficulty of writing about such things that
I suggested at the beginning of this collection. They are so fresh and
immediate, so much the living Liza. I still feel profoundly uncertain
about whether to do it or not, though. I'd like to proclaim them to

the world – but at the same time I'm reluctant even to quote from them, because she wrote them to me, and me alone, her friend of those two days and nights and the months that followed.

Her handwriting is bold and clear. The tone of this first letter, dated 4 July, is lightly conversational. She is staying with a friend in Cumberland, and there are stylised drawings of the scenery – 'beautiful'; the local inhabitants (sheep) – 'a bit dumb'; and a fellow visitor to the Lake District, said to be a member of the Leadenhall Ladies' Hiking Association, striking out across the fells with emergency rations of gin and ginger nuts peeping out of her rucksack. There is also one of herself, kneeling in a cabbage patch to lift the cover on an incinerator and check whether *sa flamme* has survived our separation. She appends a footnote: 'Hope you know your Racine & Corneille!' I do, and am almost as touched to have this further small link between us identified as to hear that so far the flame has burned shamelessly bright. But then there is another picture of her with eyes cast pensively down, and a bubble for her thought: 'Maybe it's true that IGNIS EXARDESCIT ET EXTINGUETUR CINERES MANENT HAEC VERITAS VITAE EST,' which she says she saw written up over the fireplace of an abandoned Sicilian monastery. Classical languages, unlike French, are not something I share with her. I know no Greek, and my Latin is only just about adequate to read this: 'The fire blazes up and will be extinguished; the ashes remain. This is the truth of life.' Already, in this first light-hearted letter! I wonder if for a moment I too feel the coldness of those waiting ashes.

In the six months that come first, though, there are another fifty-five letters in which the fire still burns. Allowing for the time when we don't write because we're actually together, this is about a letter every three days – and there are some periods when it's every single day. I don't have my side of the correspondence, but so far as I can reconstruct from her responses my letters are almost as frequent. We're mostly apart. In the little engagement diary for 1957 that I have managed to find there are only two actual meetings mentioned for these first few weeks: one for tea in the Pâtisserie Valerie in Soho, on the Monday after we get back from Cambridge; one with no time or place specified, only the word 'LIZA' in capital letters entirely filling the space for Friday, 19 July. Neither entry brings anything to mind.

In the meantime she is criss-crossing the North of England, honouring promises already made to stay with various friends and relatives. These next six months are going to be a story of journeys, in fact, of journeys and the letters that the journeys necessitate, and which at least leave me with some trace of what happened and what we felt. The journeys are often difficult; the letters – her letters, at any rate – are tender, funny and alive – as informal as conversation, as sharp as literature. About the 'happy–sad' of barrel-organs, for example, and 'the relentless even monotony of their gaiety'. We sometimes write to each other in French – our small private link again. She spent school holidays in Tunisia, where her family were living at the time, and her French is good – well seasoned with subjunctives. She gives me the unique present of a French text – a single typescript sheet she found on a bookstall in Tunis, with a tersely shattering poem, '*Miserere*', presumably published clandestinely in occupied France during the war under a pseudonym, René Renne, about life and death in the *maquis*, which I have never found anywhere else since.

Liza's life that emerges from the letters as they go on is not entirely easy. She is trying to devote herself to her work on the difficult course she has chosen, reading Herodotus and Thucydides in Greek, and never getting quite as far each day as she hopes; struggling to understand the philosophy of Plato and Aristotle, also in the original. And at the same time she has to meet all the social and family demands traditionally made upon women. Her father is working in Rome, and at the end of July, while her mother is in London with the younger children, she is expected to go out to cook for him and look after him. She is torn in two – a naturally good and loving daughter, but desperate to work, and, as she says, tired of being *fille de la maison*. Now I am distracting her still further – and making the confusion of her feelings even worse, because she wants to show her love by cooking for *me*.

How do I respond to this? I don't know directly what I think or feel about anything, since I don't have my side of the exchange. In the foreground of the correspondence is this vividly live woman. Somewhere, voiceless and disembodied, like the unseen figures she is reading about who are passing Plato's cave, is a man known only by the shadow he casts. His letters are typed – I've been typing everything for several years now, letters, lecture notes, essays, in preparation for my career as a journalist – which she says she doesn't mind, though she would rather like some kind of recognised formula to mark the end, such as *Veuillez agréer, Mademoiselle, l'expression de mes sentiments les plus respectueux* – and perhaps someone could lend me a pen or pencil, so that I could write at any rate my signature by hand. They make her laugh, anyway, and she carries them round everywhere, to and fro across England, in the back pocket of her jeans, to read them over and over again.

Is this invisible correspondent at all like me, the present living me, who is writing about him here? Not much, by the sound of it, because according to Liza he is all kinds of wonderful things that I am not. He also has his faults, she recognises – irresoluteness, chronic indecision, egotism – though she claims to like them. Also his Italian is very poor (I should have thought non-existent at this point). And his French pronunciation isn't good (how has she ever heard it?). And he smokes too much. Yes, he smokes. Egotism and clunky French are bad enough; how she stands the smoking I can't now imagine.

Sometimes there's no letter from him when there should be. '. . . So bitterly disappointed not to have a letter from you this morning . . .' '. . . You never write to me . . .' '. . . I'm sure you've forgotten about me . . .' Not his fault, though, usually, but the difficulties of the post, with which they are both struggling. Hard to imagine now, when electronic messages fly back and forth as fast as words spoken across a table, how people ever managed to hold any kind of dialogue at all by post. Letters take two, three days each way, and later, when she has gone to Rome, three or four days. One, misdelivered to the Vatican, takes five. Then: 'TWO letters from you . . .' When one of the correspondents is travelling it becomes almost impossible. 'No letter from you this morning. Worse still, if there *is* one tomorrow I shall have left before it arrives. Worst of all, it means I shan't hear anything from you till Monday evening when I get back from York.'

What else am I doing (if this irresolute, egotistic, but otherwise apparently wonderful phantom really is the same person as me) apart from writing these letters? Trying to teach myself shorthand, it seems, for my forthcoming career as a reporter. Also preparing for the possibility of going to see her in Rome in August. I have never been there, and she is making me read Burckhardt to find out something about Renaissance history and art, together with Tacitus (in translation, of course, unlike her) for the formal history of classical Rome, and Suetonius for its seamier side.

But *am* I going to Rome? 'You MUST come,' she writes. 'I'm getting horrider and horrider without you . . . The only danger at the moment seems to be that everyone except me may go away and you couldn't stay alone in the flat with me . . . I see my father's point about this . . . But if only you can get some money for your fare I'm sure the rest will take care of itself.'

Yes, if only I can get some money for my fare. Letters, journeys . . . and this is the third thread of the story: money. Or the lack of it. One day, when I am for some forgotten reason in Canterbury, I apparently send her three picture postcards. 'It was rather an expensive joke,' she complains, 'say 3 x 4d for the pcs and 6d in stamps. 1/6d. *Quelle extravagance!*' One and sixpence for postage and postcards is one thing; money for international travel is another. How am I going to lay my hands on it? Is this the summer I'm driving a van around the West End, delivering to Harrods, Selfridges, Fenwick's and elsewhere for an exclusive little firm in a mews just off Oxford Street, who (if I may drop a name) make the Queen's handbags? Or was the van-driving the previous summer, when I was trying to raise the fare for *that* year's trip, to Moscow? Even the years are getting confused inside my head now!

My other way of earning for the Moscow venture, not on my own behalf but as my contribution to the group of fellow undergraduates I was travelling with, had been writing articles about it for various magazines. Two of them had been comic pieces for *Punch*. It seemed to be an easy way to make money. In which case, surely, all I have to do now is a few more pieces for *Punch*, this time for my own profit, and I shall be on the train to Rome. (I don't think planes have been invented.) I can't remember how many pieces I send them, just that they are boldly confident and adventurous, now I know I have a customer waiting – and particularly now that I know my letters make Liza laugh. *Punch* rejects them all, one after another.

Not the train, then. But I make a fortunate discovery: somebody I knew at university is also on his way to Rome – is going to stay with Liza's brother Nicholas – and he has a car. All he needs is for me to get to Paris, where he happens to be, and share the driving and the cost of the petrol. A slow way of getting to Rome, before motorways – two long days – but possibly one guaranteed ride all the way is better than hitchhiking, which is how I have always got around the cities of Europe before.

So, the overnight ferry Newhaven–Dieppe for cheapness, and I arrive sleepless (once again) at the Gare Saint-Lazare in the early-August morning sunshine. A quick bowl of coffee and a croissant with my friend, who can't wait to get under way any more than I can – though in his case it's not Rome, it turns out, that's making him so impatient.

'Would you mind, Michael,' he says, 'if we make a slight diversion by way of Avignon?'

Avignon?

'Yes, because, oh, Michael, the most wonderful girl in the world lives there, and I thought we might just look in. It's not too far out of our way.'

Do I mind? Of course I mind! Do I tell him? Do I protest that the most wonderful girl in the world lives not in Avignon but in Rome? And that Avignon is in fact miles out of our way, down the old N7 through Auxerre and Lyon, whereas Rome is down the N5 through Dijon and Geneva? I probably don't. He's plainly a bit unhinged about this second most wonderful girl of his. Anyway, it's his car. A Morris Minor, but it has a sunroof, which is down for the sun to shine on us and the wind to embrace us. And driving south, whether it's down the N5 or the N7, is after all driving south.

So, Avignon. It's nearly six hundred kilometres, and with every dusty kilometre my friend gets more excited. I start to wonder uneasily whether I will ever detach him from this second most wonderful girl of his soon enough for us still to get to Rome before another night passes. By the time we reach Avignon it's dark. We drive straight to the girl's house, and I stay sitting in the car as my friend runs to the front door, unable to wait a moment longer. Five minutes later he's back. 'She left for London this morning,' he says.

We find a café terrace, where my friend slumps, broken, over a pastis in the hot Provençal night. I'm touched – he really is crazy about her! Though I can't help feeling privately relieved that we can now at any rate be sure of continuing our journey in the morning and reaching Rome before nightfall.

At last he pulls himself together. 'Tomorrow,' he says. Tomorrow – good. He's not too shattered to remember what we're supposed to be doing. 'Would you mind very much if we went via Pallanza?'

Pallanza? Where's Pallanza?

'On Lake Maggiore.'

Lake Maggiore? But wouldn't that be going northwards rather than southwards?

'A bit, but we can take a short cut through the mountains, and oh, Michael, there's a girl there I've always been in love with . . .'

So we spend the next day on the winding back roads of the French

211

and Italian Alps, labouring over passes, dropping into hidden valleys, and edging ever further north. An agreeable motoring holiday. Except that Liza is waiting for me in Rome! And I am everywhere but; in Digne-les-Bains, Savines-le-Lac and Oulx. In Bussoleno, Cossato and Borgosesia. Seven hundred kilometres from Rome and getting not closer but further away. As I said, this is a story of journeys. And money, or the lack of it. And letters, and all the messages to Liza to explain that I'm not in Rome because I'm in somewhere called Bussoleno – messages that can't be sent because emails and texts haven't yet been invented.

All day, as we wind through the mountains, my friend tells me about the girl in Pallanza, with whom he seems to be even more in love than he ever was with the one in Avignon, and I start to worry again about how long it will take me to drag him away. Night has fallen again by the time we reach Pallanza. We pull into the drive of an elegant villa overlooking the lake. They have evidently heard the sound of the car on the gravel, because the front door opens and a young woman – yes, attractive, certainly – stands on the doorstep. 'How marvellous . . . !' she cries in delighted surprise when she sees who it is getting out of the car, and runs to kiss him. I'm grudgingly relieved that this second detour has been worthwhile for one of us, at any rate. '. . . because you can be the first to congratulate me! I've just this moment got engaged!'

Next morning, in case my friend remembers any more girls he is in love with, even further off the road to Rome, I take a fair slice of my meagre reserves out of my wallet and travel the rest of the way by train.

• • •

So, Rome at last. 'THE BEST CITY IN THE WORLD,' says Liza in one of her letters, in capital letters, and nothing, either in the enchanted few weeks that follow, or in the many visits I have made to Rome since, inclines me to disagree with the judgement or even the capital letters.

And in the world's best city the best apartment must surely be the Mrosovskys', in a palazzo in Trastevere, the picturesque district across the river from the centre that nestles under the Janiculum, the eighth of the seven hills of Rome. The apartment has a balcony like the box of a theatre, overlooking a little square, the Piazza di San Calisto, full of restaurant tables. We all come out each evening, Martinis in hand, to gaze vertically down on to the spectacle of holiday Italy in summer, as the waiters and the hawkers and the street musicians force their way through the close-packed tables, the cotton dresses and bare brown skin, the roar of talk and laughter.

There's no shortage of us in the apartment, as Liza had feared. The children have invited friends, some staying, some calling, and the friends bring more friends, who mostly seem to have covered those thousand long miles from London on scooters. There is Liza's brother Nicholas, who will one day become a world authority on sea turtles. He's invited Veronica, who gave the party in the mews where Liza and I met, and who will fall in love here – not with him but with a mutual friend of all three of us who has arrived on one of the Vespas to stay in another palazzo somewhere. Then someone else who in years to come will be a colleague of mine on the *Observer* and marry a famous opera singer. Another who will write the great European novel, or try to; and on the pillion of his scooter a girl who in years to come will famously abandon husband and children to make her life in an ashram. Even at last, after I've gone, four weeks and who knows how many of the world's most wonderful girls later, my friend with the Morris Minor.

Emerging occasionally from his study to inspire a little sobering awe in this crew, like some stern Roman provincial governor surveying the shifting population he rules over, is the frightening figure Liza has come out here to serve: her father. He is the local head of Shell, which is why he is housed as splendidly as an ambassador, and probably exercises rather more power, suborning Italian MPs in Shell's interest. His face is particularly stony when he looks at me; I'm not the kind of young man he would hope to see courting his beloved daughter. Like a Roman governor, though, he can sometimes also indulge us all with unexpected largesse. One day he drives a carload of us out to have lunch in a vineyard belonging to a friend of his, in the hills around Velletri, and is the most genial and expansive company at table. Another evening he takes us all to the opera. My first opera! *Aida,* in the vast ruined Baths of Caracalla, where in summer the Rome Opera sings in the open air. In the instant between Aida's finishing her '*O patria mia*' and reaping the applause she is pre-empted by the summer night itself. A bright shooting star crosses the sky overhead, and instead of applauding the audience breathes a soft surprised sigh of wonder.

And then . . . Liza herself. She hasn't given up on me while I was in Savines-le-Lac or Borgosesia and left for London, or got engaged to someone else, as some of the world's other most wonderful girls have been doing before my travelling companion could reach them. She is there, in the apartment, at the opera, not just words on paper now but her whole self, visible and tangible. It's the first time we've actually been in the same piece of space together since those two first night-days in London, apart from the teashop in Soho two days later, and whatever it was that 'LIZA' in the engagement diary for Friday, 19 July signified. What's it like, actually being with her now after all our waiting? It's harder to say exactly than it was when we were apart, because being together means there are no letters from her, and in Rome for the first time, between her last letter on 12 August and her next on 8 September, I now have no written record. I expect she is still trying to keep up her daily portions of Thucydides and Aristotle. Cooking for her father – and now, probably, also for everyone else in the apartment. Do I help her? Boil the pasta, at least, and wash up? I can't remember it. When I asked Veronica recently what she recalled, the only contribution of mine to the housekeeping was my spilling soup down the wallpaper. I was extremely contrite, she assured me, and it was easily cleaned.

What does she look like, Liza, now I can see her? Suntanned, certainly, full-bosomed, smiling beneath the mass of dark hair. When I think of her I see her wearing a soft white cotton dress, as the Roman girls do on their Vespas and Lambrettas. I suspect that actually she is more likely to be wearing the practical jeans she was wearing in England, with back pockets for my letters. Though perhaps, now I'm not writing letters, she doesn't need the pockets. Not that I can always see what she's wearing, because her parents have given her a Lambretta, which she doesn't like driving herself, so she teaches me to instead, and we ride around the best city in the world in the August sunshine, like Gregory Peck and Audrey Hepburn in *Roman Holiday*, with her perched on the back, side-saddle, the way the Roman girls do when their boyfriends are with them, a scarf over her wild hair in the wind (this was long before crash helmets), and her sunburned arms round me to hold on. Has nobody thought to tell me I've died and gone to heaven?

So this is how we get away from the Thucydides and the Plato and everyone in the apartment, how we have our hours alone together, and how I first see Rome – on the Lambretta. We arrange to creep out of our bedrooms each morning while everyone else is still asleep and the air is cool, and away we go. Labouring in low gear up on to the Janiculum – gazing out over the panorama of the city into the eye of the morning sun – then swooping down past the Vatican and St Peter's, across the river into that battered and bewitching tumult of stone heads and fountains, of high ceilings and narrow alleys, of vast canvases and fallen columns, of *carabinieri* and beggars and inscriptions and excavations, of heavenward-cast eyes and blood-soaked martyrdoms. Liza tells me about Bernini and Borromini, about Domitian and Diocletian, the Borghese and the Doria Pamphili, and instils in me a lifelong prejudice against Caravaggio. Back to Trastevere for lunch and a siesta, then sometimes out again to scooter down to the coast and swim at Ostia or Fregene, as far north as Civitavecchia.

Do any of the others realise what's going on? How could they not? Her father does, I know. When I asked Veronica what she remembered about those sunlit weeks, she said she had had no idea that Liza and I had been in love. But then I had had no idea about her and the mutual friend of ours whom she would eventually marry. I suppose we were all a little too preoccupied with our own feelings.

Things can't have been quite as simply idyllic as I remember them now. After I've gone and our letters resume Liza talks about having been 'petulant and irritable and childish in just the way you hate'. I have made her intensely happy quite often, she says, 'even if we do quarrel'. So she's sometimes been upset? I've sometimes reacted badly? We've sometimes quarrelled? I have no recollection of any of it.

It's over soon enough, anyway, and I'm on my way back to England – to Manchester, to start my career and the rest of my life. Another journey, by train all the way this time, paid for, I suppose, with the last of my money. The seeing-off at the station is evidently a wretched occasion. We were 'horrid' to each other, says Liza afterwards, and it sounds from the way she puts it as if I've already described it in much the same way myself. Or that *he* has, that same old shadow on the wall of the cave who has now reappeared. In all the disconsolation of the day, apparently, he has – *I* have – managed to leave behind the picnic Liza has prepared for me. So now she is back in the Piazza di San Calisto, choking miserably on 'Michael's' cheese and 'Michael's' mortadella, while I am on the train north with nothing to eat – and no seat, either, standing in the corridor for twenty-three hours to Paris, then three more from Paris to Calais. Another sleepless journey. Not that I get much sympathy from Liza when I tell her. I should be harder about travel if I'm a journalist, she says with unaccustomed sharpness. 'A novelist perhaps can be complaining about third class travel, but I imagine journalists as able to do *anything* and endure *any* physical hardship.' Maybe this is what encourages me some years later to start writing novels.

I'm not sure why she is so suddenly stern. Nor is she very sympathetic over what happens on the next stage of the journey, when, after some twenty-six waking hours on my feet, I find the cross-Channel ferry is full as well. In the crowd on deck I come across a girl I knew slightly at Cambridge, and we go to have a drink together in the hope of escaping the press of bodies. We find we have started out in opposite directions. I show her the arrow to the bar. 'That's the third-class bar,' she says, 'and it will be just as bad as here. More sensible to try the first-class.' I have to confess that I've only got a third-class ticket. 'So have I,' she says. 'It doesn't matter.'

There is indeed rather more room in the first-class bar, perhaps even a hope of sitting down, and I follow her fearfully, expecting at any moment to be arrested and imprisoned. I have just bought us both glasses of something restorative when the ticket inspector comes into the bar. The first thing his eye falls on is us. I show him my ticket. His lip curls a little, and he indicates the door, then turns to my companion. She has somehow become a little girl, I discover – the kind of little girl who has been brought up by nannies and governesses. 'My daddy's got my ticket,' she lisps artlessly, 'and he's in one of the cabins being sick.' The ticket inspector touches his cap respectfully, then waits to make sure I am out of the door. And that's the last I see of any space to sit down, or my posh friend, or my drink.

• • •

So now I am in rainy, grimy, red-brick Manchester, starting my new life, and I have forgotten Liza. Or so she complains, in Rome still, as her side of our correspondence resumes. The evenings there are getting cooler, she reports, and the glare is off the buildings, so that the detail on them glows. The last of my fellow guests have left, and she is getting down to some serious Herodotus and Plato at last, then packing, and tearing up all her old love letters ('*except* yours') in preparation for coming back herself. I haven't forgotten her, in spite of my new distractions, as she realises when at last my letters start to arrive again. On the contrary – I am apparently *begging* her to come and visit me in Manchester before she goes up to Oxford for the start of term, and reproaching her because she has agreed to stay on to look after her father in the empty flat, then to come back, not by train, but by car with him, slowly, stopping off in various grand hotels on the way.

I can't help being touched now, re-reading her letters as a father of daughters myself, by what a devoted daughter she is, and by what pride and pleasure her father obviously takes in her company. They stay longest in Milan, in a particularly luxurious hotel, and she has to be charming to all kinds of relatives and her father's business acquaintances. It makes her feel terribly mixed up, she says.

> Here I am dressed in my best clothes, with stockings, and powder and lipstick on, and jewels, all set to be the rich oil magnate's idle daughter, who has a car at her disposal, does a little desultory sightseeing, has *huge* expensive meals several times a day and has never made her own bed, or polished her shoes. But in fact I'm a down-at-heel student desperately trying to plough through a syllabus far beyond her powers, and worse still in love with a journalist far away in Manchester, of all places.

Then finally she is back in Oxford, and is once again the real down-at-heel, hard-working self she feels herself to be. We are still kept apart by 160 miles of damp, autumnal England. So, more letters – and difficult to know how we find the time. We've both got things to occupy us. The Greek classics at the Oxford end, and at the other my new life of full-time professional writing. There's a lot of literature that has survived from classical Athens, and a lot of reportable world radiating out from present-day Manchester: the effects of full employment on local pawnbrokers and of sewage on the Tyne;

the last steam locomotive to be built at Doncaster; Jodrell Bank's attempts to use their new radio telescope to track sputnik, the world's first satellite; not to mention local house fires and traffic accidents.

The letters fly back and forth, nevertheless. Or at any rate trudge, at pre-digital speeds. And now there are the journeys again as well, which are harder to manage. She can only get permission from her tutor for one weekend away during the term, and that by lying, something she doesn't find easy. She does come, on a train that seems reluctant to be involved in the deception – or rather three trains, from Oxford to Birmingham after her last class, from Birmingham to Stafford, and one from Stafford that finally reaches Manchester around midnight. We shut ourselves away from the cold and damp for a day or two in the little attic studio flat I've found, that smells of coal gas and bacon grease, with a pale view of the cotton mills of Oldham through the industrial haze. I go to Oxford a few times in my turn, though that way round, for some reason, you have to follow a different route, and travel not just all evening but all night. A train that clanks unenthusiastically through the industrial history of the Black Country in the small hours, until it can no longer postpone reaching the desolate elevated pre-dawn emptiness of Wolverhampton High Level. Down the stairs to the less elevated desolation of Wolverhampton Low Level, and a train to Birmingham Snow Hill. A walk across the centre of the city, where the first few early risers are beginning to stir in the streets, and with them some hope of daylight and returning life, to Birmingham New Street, and at last a train to Oxford, the destination I dimly remember setting out for the previous day, and where I arrive as estranged from normal reality as Liza and I both were that very first night-day in Cambridge.

Letters and journeys, journeys and letters . . . And the third thread of the story still: money, or the dearth of it. I think I'm getting twelve guineas a week when I start on the *Guardian* – Liza's worried that I'm not eating enough – and in Oxford I have to have somewhere to stay. She eventually finds me a room near the station for 10/6d a night. Even so I'm reduced to borrowing money off her, I don't know how much, or whether I ever repay it, only that she is horrified I still end up with so little left, and says I should have borrowed more.

She comes to Manchester a few times in the vacation, when she doesn't have to ask permission. Trains, money and tutors, though, are evidently not the only difficulties of these brief times together. 'Last weekend was wonderful,' she writes after one, but after another: 'It's awful having these weekends that only go right at the end . . .' And 'I always seem to write horrid letters after I've seen you.' I apparently write nostalgically loving ones, though they're not always quite to her taste: 'No more carnal reminiscences, please.'

Then again, a weekend that she says was one of the happiest times of her life. We even seem to have discussed marriage at some point, and perhaps it's this that began to bring us up against our limitations. 'I love you more than anyone else in the world,' she writes, 'but I don't love you enough to marry you at the moment. And I doubt I ever shall.'

This is one of the things that moves me most as I read her letters now – her truth to herself. Already in September, when she was still in Rome, a week or so after I'd left, she was agreeing with some self-deprecating assessment that I must have made of my contribution to her life. 'Yes, you *haven't* done much for me. In fact you've taken most of my energy since July, to the detriment of my work, character, looks, and good temper.' The inclusion of the last three areas suggests that she was not being entirely serious. But about the work I think she was. And as that autumn goes on she understands more and more clearly how important it is to her, just as mine is to me. We haven't exchanged more than a few journeys back and forth before she is thinking of ending them: 'I seriously considered writing to you and saying I'd better not see you ever again, because Greats was more important to me than you.'

Yet nothing, it turns out, is really that simple for her, and she follows the bewildering contradictions and changes of her feelings just as truthfully. She won't come to Manchester for the vacation – but then she does, at any rate for a weekend, and it's a particularly happy time – 'more familiar . . . and just *further* along the road towards knowing each other'. Then her next journey is to Rome for Christmas, and everything there is even more tangled: lovely to be back in the old familiar world – and being at home grates more than ever – and there's no Greek dictionary in the house to work with – and she's wishing she was married to me – and she's not coming to Manchester when she comes back – and she loves me more than ever. 'Why must I be so teenager?' she says.

A roller coaster; but now, as on any roller coaster, you can begin to feel that the overall trajectory is downward. The following letter ends with a little drawing of her, body all heart and face all tears, together with another little drawing of us holding hands and contemplating each other. 'Liza loves Michael,' says the caption. 'Michael anyway used to love Liza.'

Yes, he did love Liza, this shadowy Michael, who may have become me as the years have passed. And maybe she's right, that he doesn't love her quite so much any longer. One way or another the end is approaching, and he seems to be the one who actually wields the blade because her next letter is a stoical and graceful acceptance that it's over. There is a lot of sadness, a lot of tears – but just possibly, in the midst of it all, you can detect a certain measure of relief. 'We couldn't possibly go on at the pace we were going. Flights and droves of letters, long journeys, Manchester, Rome, Oxford. It's simply not practical.'

What has he actually said in the fatal letter? Something, apparently, about her not entering his intellectual world. What intellectual world is this? The world of Salford pawnbrokers and Newcastle sewage? It can't have been *this* Michael, can it – *me* – who uttered such a pompous and arrogant putdown? I suppose it was. She might have replied that I seemed to be rather left outside *her* intellectual world of Plato and Herodotus. In any case, as she says, you don't get married on the basis of intellectual compatibility but something else, something intangible, something that she sees is irrevocably missing between us. We were almost there, she thinks. But not quite. She, in spite of everything, wants to marry me – *desperately* wants to marry me. 'But you don't want to marry me. You honestly don't love me enough. And you know best what is right for yourself.'

It's January, the bleak depths of winter, almost exactly six months after that sweltering June night when we first met. I take the desolate overnight train to Oxford one last time to talk everything through with her face to face, and she writes the last two of those fifty-six letters that speak to me so strongly when I re-read them after all these years. They contain a few reproaches, but not many. They're mostly sad but loving. 'I feel exactly the same about you, but I accept my sorrow, and no longer fight it. I feel strangely relaxed and strong.' She is selling the Lambretta, that steed of the gods on which we soared through Rome together in the August sunshine, and she sends me what she calls a small love-present, *Daphnis and Chloe*, the Arcadian tale – 'pagan, gentle, idyllic' – by the late Latin author Longus, of a goatherd and a shepherdess and their love. Not really us, perhaps, a goatherd and a shepherdess. 'But I feel calm like the story about our 6 months love,' she says. 'It was good while it lasted.'

And the very last words of the very last letter: 'Write to me some time.'

I never do.

• • •

Over sixty years go by, and though I never write, never catch a glimpse of her and never hear from her again, I have some idea how much I owe her, and not only for introducing me to Rome and its history. I certainly haven't forgotten her, and I put a little of her into a character in one of my novels – a touch of her gentleness and straightforwardness, though the character in the story is learning deportment at a finishing school, not reading Classics at Oxford.

At some point in the last twenty years or so I must have extracted her letters from the general muddle of correspondence in my files, and put them in chronological order in a folder of their own, because they're waiting for me when I come to write these pieces, and when Claire, my wife, challenges the absence of women. I open the folder, and there she is again as she always was, at still no more than postal distance. Gentle and straightforward, yes. In love for the first time, serious and hard-working, and torn by all the conflicting demands made upon her. I have to recognise how honest and clear-sighted she is in her account of our feelings, and to accept that we are right to end it. So perhaps I shouldn't reproach myself too much now for being the one who actually said the words. Perhaps it was better, too, to make a clean break and never to be in touch again. I can't help being uneasily aware, though, that a year later I was in love with someone else who was a much less probable partner than Liza – and this time was actually getting engaged to her – and breaking off even more painfully. A bit of a pattern here, perhaps. Which recurs, I have to confess, before I finally settle totally with my second wife to forty years of constancy. So Liza is well shot of me.

Perhaps I should get in touch with her at last, though, I think as I read her letters, even sixty years late. If I can find her. I do some research, and think finally of the lifelong connection that was symbolised by the way my fellow graduands and I held on to our tutor's fingers that summer's day so long ago. And yes, there in the back-numbers of the Somerville College magazine, I find her. Four years too late. She died in 2016.

I feel a quite unforeseen sadness. Perhaps my original reluctance to say anything about the relationships of love rather than of friendship was right. This once was enough – more than enough; I shan't try it again. *Ignis exardescit et extinguetur*, as the old monks wrote over their fireplace in Sicily, and Liza quoted in that very first letter, a lifetime ago; the fire blazes up and will be extinguished. The ashes that remain are too sad to contemplate. *Haec veritas vitae est.*

• • •

Or is it?

Attached to the magazine's obituary is the photograph of her – the first one I have ever seen. It was taken probably when she was in her sixties, and she is just as beautiful as ever. She seems to radiate serenity and goodness. The obituarist speaks of her warmth, generosity and understanding.

She became a lawyer after she graduated, it says, then a teacher, then took diplomas in social studies at LSE and became a social worker in Tower Hamlets and Haringey, which I should think was a pretty tough option. She married a paediatrician, Jonathan Shaw, a consultant at University College Hospital, and they had three children.

Then, in her sixties, she took another degree – in Russian. I imagine that this came out of a growing interest in her forebears, and in particular her late father, Peter Mrosovsky, the imposing patriarch who had exercised such dominion over the household in the Piazza di San Calisto, and, as viceroy of mighty Shell, over all Rome. He was a more complex figure than I had realised, and in her later years Liza became an authority on his life. His background was Russian, despite his Polish surname. From a learned article that she published shortly before her death I discover that he had begun his life in St Petersburg, supposedly the son of a landscape painter, in fact the illegitimate son of a well-known Italian baritone. By training he was a chemist, and he had worked for Shell in Romania, where Liza was born, and in Tunisia. Before that, though, he had had literary connections. During his holidays from Bedales, where he had been sent to school – the one fixed point in a peripatetic childhood – he was fostered by a famous poet, Edward Thomas, and met another, Robert Frost. As an undergraduate at Cambridge he had smuggled an early copy of the forbidden *Ulysses* into Britain, and read parts of it aloud to a friend of his, a fellow undergraduate at Trinity. The friend was Vladimir Nabokov, who later established Peter Mrosovsky in the canon of modern literature by making him, as Liza shows in her paper (in spite of Nabokov's own denials), a model for one of the characters in his early novel *Glory*.

Now here I am, trying to find a small corner in the world of words for Liza herself – and to do it with the help of some of her own words in those fifty-six letters. Who owns those words now? Her husband, probably, since he is still alive. I wrote to him to ask his permission to quote from them, and I showed him what I had written. He in his turn showed it to their three daughters, and he responded on behalf of all of them with a warmth and generosity that I found very moving. Strange to think that neither this long and happy marriage nor their three daughters would have existed, any more than my own marriages and three daughters would, if the possible future we discussed had been realised, and the *exardescit* had not been followed by the *extinguetur*. True, *cineres manent*, but among the ashes are sometimes written words and memories that are not cold at all but still warm, the way ashes stay for so long. And, in any case, from the ashes of the past other fires flare up in their turn, and the heat and light they radiate shape the world as it has actually turned out to be, with all the beloved partners and children, all the friends and acquaintances, who have made us what we are. Perhaps this is the real truth of life, or closer to it.

Mantower

This particular story begins, like the story of man in the Bible, with a fall.

In this case, though, the man was just me and the fall was painfully literal. I got up for a pee in the middle of the night, and found myself, not escorted out of Eden by God's security people, but lying on the hard tiled floor beside the lavatory, with several broken ribs and no idea how I'd arrived there.

It started me thinking about things, as I got over the initial shock and all the tests and scans in the weeks that followed. About how old I seemed to have got all of a sudden. This was some years ago now – I've got a lot older since. About all the life that had led up to being so old and all the people around me who'd shaped that life. How old we'd all got! A lot of us, in fact – even people the same age as me or younger – were already dead. More of us have died since. I think that this was one of the things that started me making these sketches of some of them, while I remained among the survivors.

But how long would that last?

I was evidently more fragile than I'd supposed. And I started to think about the strange organism that all this performance depended upon: my own body.

• • •

My midnight fall, for a start. What surprised me most about it, now I'd begun to think about it objectively, was not so much that I'd fallen but that I'd ever managed to remain upright. For nearly eighty years a structure just over six feet high had balanced for a good part of each day on a base about ten inches long by four inches wide at its widest. How long would David have stayed upright, exquisitely proportioned as he was, if Michelangelo had not fixed him to his plinth? Or any of the other marble and bronze figures who stand about with such assurance in our cities? The ground would be strewn with horizontal kings and generals, with gods and mothers of gods, and all around them a detritus of detached marble heads and shattered limbs.

Or think about it as architecture. If I'd been constructed to the same standards as a modern tower block there would have been another foot or more of me concreted into the bathroom floor. To put it the other way round, if the high-rise buildings that now dominate the London skyline had been built to the same proportions as me they would be not fifty floors high, or even seventy-eight, like the Shard, but something more like a hundred – postmodernist whimsies bulging outwards from their narrowest point, and plonked down on the bare earth without foundations. Somewhat fewer than eighty years, I think, would have elapsed before the wind had got up, or some passer-by had brushed against them. And if they'd had not only to stand still but to move around, as I've spent my life doing . . . over ground full of potholes and kerbs . . . groping their way out to the bathroom, half-asleep, in the dark . . .

It's not the first time, of course, that this particular tower has fallen down. It fell down most often, curiously, in its early years, when it was still only half its present height or less. But it's the first time it's done it since those early days without any external cause to explain it – ice underfoot, an unnoticed step, soap or (on one occasion) my daughter's dog being chased by another dog. For nearly eighty years a complex internal machinery has evidently been at work without my ever noticing it, sensing ground levels and wind speeds, motion forwards, backwards and sideways, estimating the turning moment of rucksacks and babes in arms, then finely adjusting muscle tensions to compensate.

So, I'm looking down on myself from a hundred floors up. From this height perspective makes my feet look even smaller – about one inch long, I estimate, if I compare them with a ruler at eye level. Toy feet. Piffling appendages. I've always had some faint apprehension of how hard the departments on the middle floors work, pumping away day and night, gasifying, detoxifying, digesting. I hadn't really thought about what was happening on the lower floors. Nothing much, I'd assumed, if one was standing still. But even here, I realise now, the staff are on duty, endlessly monitoring the information coming in from the nervous system about surrounding conditions, and doing whatever's necessary to adapt to them.

Until one day their efforts are brushed aside by a sudden surge of uncompensated gravity, as abruptly as democracy in a military putsch. No ice, no soap; you simply go for a pee, just as you have so many times in your life before, and in the half-darkness of the urban night and the half-conscious confusion of half-waking, the now elderly operatives downstairs are caught napping.

I'm not the only one that this kind of thing happens to. Half of all the people of my age, according to NHS Direct, fall down at least once a year. Bamber told me, in the last few years of his life, that he fell down about once a week. And for many people it has

much worse results than a few broken ribs and a sudden awareness
of how implausible the whole human arrangement is; it's the most
common cause of death in older people.

A surgeon told a friend of mine that rule number one for healthy
living in old age is: always hold on to the handrail when you're
going downstairs. Better still might be to get a builder to bolt you
to a plinth or cement you deep into the bedrock.

• • •

You don't usually look down at the building below you from the
boardroom windows up here on the top floor. What you see most
of the time is all the other towers around you. About some of them
you know considerably more than you do about yourself – not just
what they look like round the front, from head height, but seen
from behind, seen from above, seen from ground level. With one
of them at least, probably, you know what each inch of their fabric
feels like to the touch. Then the overnight catastrophe happens, and
when you've got yourself upright again and daylight has returned,
it occurs to you to open the window, lean out and look down to see
what's been going on below.

A hundred floors! And all occupied by the same firm! A hundred trillion cells, as my cousin Keith Frayn, who's a biochemist,
once worked out for me when I asked him, all labouring away at
their own specialities, all organising and reorganising themselves
in complex alliances and hierarchies. I'm the managing director
of this great conglomerate, and I'm only now, after eighty years
of almost unbroken good health, beginning to be surprised at the

immense variety of activities and specialist skills for which I'm nominally responsible.

I've never even noticed how much routine maintenance I've had to put into it. At each meal, according to usually reliable sources on the internet, I've taken in about five hundred grams of food – a kilogram or so a day – and excreted about the same amount. So, in the thirty thousand days I've spent on this earth, about thirty tons of stuff have passed through my digestive system, which is equivalent to the weight of seven elephants. Seven elephants in; seven elephants out. I've apparently also drunk, and passed, about a litre of fluid a day. That's thirty thousand litres – almost enough to fill a twenty-metre swimming pool.

I've also, of course, been breathing – breathing without cease, 23,000 times a day. With each breath I've extracted about 350 millilitres of air from the atmosphere, and returned the same amount. So that in the course of my life I've apparently passed some 245 million litres of air through my lungs – enough to fill nearly fifty gas holders.

Most of the architecture I'm looking down on seems elegantly fit for purpose. Two legs – a very reasonable number. One less and I should have had to hop everywhere, and would surely have suffered my great fall many years earlier; three or more and I should have been faced with an endless succession of wearisome choices about which to step forward with next. Two arms – also perfect, or how else should I have held a knife and fork, or opened a can of sardines? (Though a third, and even a fourth and a fifth, might have come in handy for wallpapering, say, or for holding screwdriver, screw and whatever you're trying to join together.) But the arbitrariness of some of the other features is odd. Why ten fingers, for instance? Why ten toes? All those nails to trim, when forefinger and thumb alone and two feet without any appendages at all would surely have been enough for most purposes.

Halfway up the facade, if you happen to be male, there's one particularly weird anomaly. I realise that you've got to have a projecting feature of some sort if you're going to make sexual reproduction work, and maybe its disconcertingly wild variations in length and flexibility, from a floppy half-inch at one moment to, at the next, a steel-reinforced tower in its own right, a dozen or so times as long, may be necessary to combine function and security, though why we up here on the top floor have so dismayingly little control over these variations is hard to understand. But what in heaven's name is going on with the siting of the testicles? How can something so essential to the survival of the species, so easily injured and so sensitive to pain, have been left by evolution dangling outside the fortifications? I look down from the boardroom and am astonished, now I see them with fresh eyes, to realise that the kind of thing most companies keep in a safe – the personal details of the staff and the plans for future development – this company keeps in a bag suspended outside the windows of the forty-ninth floor. Knowing that if anyone handles it roughly – the window cleaners, say, bashing it against their cradle – the whole building is going to jackknife in agony.

Nothing I can do now to correct this extraordinary freak of natural selection but draw a veil of protective trousering over it. But how did accidents and the competition of rivals not haul such a hostage to so many different aspects of fortune back into the safety of the building millions of years before trousers were even invented?

• • •

What I start to notice next are the small private variations from the norm that make this particular body personal to me – some of them there from birth, some acquired over the next eighty years. My feet, to start with the devices that so improbably keep the whole structure upright. Even more improbably in my case, because mine are seriously defective. They pronate – the soles slope up towards the centre, so that the actual load-bearing area of each one is even smaller than it should be. By my calculation they carry the best part of twice the weight per square inch of the most implausibly balanced creature I can think of in the rest of the natural world – a big bird like a goose, say, with one leg tucked up beneath it, standing on the other to rest.

There's another problem, too: my feet aren't level with each other, because my left leg is shorter than my right, so that if my body weren't somehow taking up the slack the whole skyscraper would be as way out of plumb as the Leaning Tower of Pisa. Now think of those unanchored high-rises tottering around London in the dark, not only without foundations but balanced on a ground floor that was several per cent out of the horizontal . . . So skilfully does the body compensate for even such gross discrepancies as this, though, that in my case sixty years went by before anyone noticed.

On top of my right foot, still just visible in a slanting evening light, is my one extant scar, the last trace of a hot summer afternoon some seventy-five years ago, when I was running in and out of the freezing spray from a garden hose in a friend's garden and fell over the prong of an upturned garden fork. There would be a lot of other scars all over me marking the history of my life if the body were not as adept at concealing lesions as the earth at burying old wars. If I'd made a time-lapse film of all the scratches, bruises, spots, boils and rashes that have come and gone on my skin over the last eighty years, all the

237

holes made by pins, splinters, thorns and insects, by needles extracting blood or injecting vaccines, it would look like soup simmering.

Other battles, largely invisible to the rest of the world, have been fought beneath the surface. Ferocious skirmishing at various times up and down my digestive tract. A major local war in my lower back, which broke out with bewildering suddenness on Tuesday, 14 December 1976, during a game of squash, and continued through an era of intermittent strife as long as the Thirty Years War, subsiding (though fighting still flares up from time to time) only when the irregularities in the length of my legs and the level of the soles of my feet were discovered, and orthotics prescribed to correct them.

Most of these problems had explicable causes. Some of the other anomalies and irregularities are baffling, and it's difficult to know whether they're personal idiosyncrasies or the kind of thing that everyone suffers from. On my upper left thigh is a bit of me that seems to have died several decades prematurely: a patch of skin without feeling, as if it had been injected by the dentist with novocaine, as alien to me as the insensate leg that Oliver Sacks's patient tried to throw out of bed. Then in the area above my coccyx for the last ten years or so I've had an itch, with no visible cause. Long, irregular scratches appear quite frequently higher up my back, on and between my shoulder blades, as mysteriously as crop circles. Much more tedious are the cramps that so often in the night seize various parts of my legs like a torturer's pincers. The worst are in the big muscles of the thigh, the second worst in the calf. I hurl myself out of bed with amazing speed, because the only treatment is to load one's full weight on to the affected leg. In my haste my feet get tangled in the bedclothes – it's surprising that no ribs have so far got broken like this – and the few seconds' delay makes me wonder once again how anyone ever endures serious lasting pain. Sometimes the lightning strikes my toes, or my fingers. A new development is cramp in my shins. This isn't so painful, perhaps because there are surely no muscles in your shins to get cramped – but since by the same token there are none to get uncramped, it's harder to get rid of.

And I choke, almost as readily as I breathe. I choke on toast, pepper, vinaigrette, water – any food, any drink. My own saliva. A mouthful of air; air is particularly dangerous. Choking often leads to sneezing at the same time. It's surprising that I haven't choked or sneezed to death a long time before this falling-over business began.

Do other people bite their own tongue as often as I do when they eat? Odd, if so. You'd think that if we'd managed to evolve ways of differentiating between food and tongue at all, as we seem to have done, then evolution would by now have perfected them, because being suddenly unable to eat or speak in the middle of a meal would surely have reduced an individual's probability of survival, or at least of attracting sexual partners.

• • •

Difficult to know what's going on in the inner chambers of the building, except by inference from vague sensations and external symptoms. I've had two rare direct glimpses, though, when the doctors put a television camera up my behind to check the state of my colon. Alan Bennett, in the wonderful section of *Untold Tales* about his own experiences in the lower intestine, says he was given Valium, and he rather enjoyed its effects. I don't recall any drugs, but I was kept entertained like a bored child by being allowed to watch television – the live broadcast from the camera as it tracked further and further into the depths of me. Seven elephant-loads of material had passed this way over the years, but there was no sign of this prodigious industry in the travelogue from my colon, since the whole thing had been cleared out first by an enema, like a factory being smartened up for a royal visit. On and on the camera went, its headlight illuminating nothing but more and more soft, moist, pink cavern, yard after yard, mile after mile, until my interest waned, and the investigators' with it.

A floor or two up and we come to the firm's central pumping and oxygenation unit, through which the fifteen gas holders of air have come and gone. I'm not sure I'd want a tour here, even if it were possible. I've never liked to think about my heart beating, or the blood going round, in case self-consciousness made me suddenly lose the trick, rather as my fingers sometimes find, if I stop to think about it, that they've forgotten which keys to press to enter my PIN or open the garden gate.

There's another little oddity in the functioning of my lungs. Fifteen breaths a minute for all these years – something over 6 billion breaths in all – and most of them I've scarcely noticed. Very occasionally, though, I think when I return to my conscious self after I've been lost in thought for a while, I've found myself taking a single much deeper one. I imagine there's a perfectly plausible physical explanation for this; my breathing had probably slowed while I was abstracted and once normal service was resumed the body was calling for extra oxygen. That deep breath, though, always had a slightly wistful feel, like a sigh, as if I were reluctant to abandon my reverie and face the everyday world again.

240

Is this part of the human condition or is it yet another mad idio-syncrasy of my own? A year or two ago I noticed that the pattern had changed. I'd begun to take these deep breaths much more fre-quently – perhaps once every five or ten minutes. An occasional trip to the land of faerie, followed by emergency oxygen, may or may not be normal, but its happening every five or ten minutes surely can't be. And now my breathing seems to have reverted to what it was before. Which is just as weird, though perhaps a good thing. Unless it means that I'm simply thinking less.

• • •

So we come to my head, the part of me which is conducting this examination. It's also the part that the rest of the world has always known best. At any rate the front of it, my face. It's my identity card. Me, for most everyday purposes. Also the running newscast that signals – consciously or unconsciously, truthfully or with intent to deceive – what mood I'm in and what I think about the person I'm talking to.

Do other people see the same familiar face that I see myself in reflections and photographs? Not at all. What I see is someone who knows he's being inspected. What they see, most of the time, is the face that I sometimes catch a glimpse of in a photograph that I didn't know was being taken, or in a reflection that I for a moment didn't realise was a reflection. Someone who's disconcertingly like me, but not me as I know me. I usually recognise him when I come across him, since I've met him quite often over the years – but in the way that I might recognise any other rather distant acquaintance.

The discrepancy between my reflection and my photograph is particularly marked in my case because my face, like my shoulders and the length of my legs, is cut on the slant. I don't notice the anomaly until I see a photograph of myself, where the deviation from the norm that I'm so familiar with in the reflected image is turned back to front. Maybe other people don't notice it so much, either, since they've probably never looked at me in the mirror. I find it a bit embarrassing, but also touching, because I've seen it before, in an old portrait of my maternal grandmother.

My nose in the middle of all this is unremarkable, except that it runs all the time. When I'm choking, coughing and sneezing, certainly, but even when I'm not. Why? Old men's noses just do, says the friend who falls down a lot, though his doesn't, and mine always has, even when it belonged to a younger man. To a boy, even, when I had various holes drilled inside it as storm drains, which all closed up again almost immediately. What a nose! Able to withstand any punishment the doctors could inflict upon it! On it ran. And runs. And no doubt ever will – run and run, longer than any of my plays, longer even than *The Mousetrap*.

My ears now have little hearing aids tucked behind them – and I still find it hard to make sense of what emerges from them. I can't understand films or plays in the few foreign languages I'm supposed to know. Nor American ones, for that matter. Nor, often, British ones. But then I can't understand much of what people say in any language, even when they're not half a mile away on a stage, or expressing themselves in cryptic neologisms on the screen. Is this the failing of my ears, or my brain?

The organs I'm using now, of course, as I look down at myself from the top of the building, are my eyes. They've never been good,

242

and my astigmatism, invisible in itself, has had a greater effect on my appearance over the years than all my other bodily defects and accidents put together. The clumsy constructions I've had to wear to keep two therapeutically distorting windows between me and the world have seemed to characterise me. As soon as I got my first pair of specs, when I was six, the little Amazon who ran the gang that assembled in the shrubbery at school every break identified me as what was then called a boffin and appointed me gang scientist, with the task of producing weapons of mass destruction. Complete strangers have sometimes since addressed me as 'doctor'. When they saw my specs on the author photograph in a theatre programme or inside the back flap of a book, people were readier to believe that I did actually know something about subjects like physics or philosophy.

I look at myself in old photographs, and there, in the changing shape of my spectacles alone, my biography is written. In childhood the lenses are small and round, in wire frames. As I grow taller the diameter of the lenses increases to match. The disapproving condescension of adolescence is framed in serious tortoiseshell, the lightheartedness of being an undergraduate by transparent plastic. As I leave university and start work the top of the frame becomes opaque, as if attempting a first frown of dawning responsibility. I begin appearing on television, and for a while the frames are huge and horn-rimmed with self-importance to keep up with all the other ambitious young men of the time. I settle down to marriage and family, and the frames of my spectacles become transparent again. Then they go silver. I don't know what that signifies. In later life they become even more understated, and I like to think that the unframed lenses say nothing about me at all. Himmler and

Dr Crippen probably thought the same. Then I have my cataracts done and even the lenses go, so that I change out of all recognition, even my own. After Bamber said goodbye to his cataracts and spectacles it took me months to feel I actually knew the stranger he had become.

My vision is effectively closed down completely from time to time without apparent cause or warning by a swirling fairground of coloured lights, which I think must be the 'aura' that migraine sufferers describe, though not, thank God, the headaches and nausea that they endure as well. Flickering illuminated wheels seem to revolve and interlock, without ever quite becoming resolved as specific images, and I have to stop working, or reading or driving until the whole circus has packed up and moved out of town, as silently and mysteriously as it arrived.

Just me, this? Or something as common as the common cold?

• • •

Hidden somewhere beneath the surface here is the most mysterious and elusive of all my body parts, the concealed control centre which is directing and coordinating everything that's happening or has ever happened, around it and on the floors below. It's conducting this survey. It's thinking these thoughts – this very one now – and directing my fingers to write these lines – this very sentence in which I'm saying it is.

Or so I believe. I have no direct evidence of its existence, no proprioception of it, in the way that I do of so many other parts of my body. An occasional headache over the years has suggested that there's something going on in there, but what it tells me is even more oblique than what a stomach ache tells me about the functioning of my digestive system. The little that I know about it I infer from the actions that my hands, feet and vocal chords undertake at its behest, and from the existence of a world around me that I know I can be aware of only if I have some very sophisticated piece of equipment somehow translating and integrating certain vibrations in the light and in the air, certain aspects of the local chemistry.

And yet it is in this unreachable, unknowable inner chamber that I instinctively feel my real self to be located. Perhaps this is simply because of its proximity to my eyes and ears. If these were in my feet instead of my head things might be different. For a start, my feet would appear to me to be large and my body would taper away upwards to the insignificant and apparently functionless protrusion on my shoulders, only an inch or two long. I should know all about the ground I walked on, be on familiar terms with worms and beetles, be more deft at avoiding puddles and dogshit. I should study every slightest change in the expression of the other feet around me. If we all had our mouths down here as well we should kiss and whisper together at ground level, and never drop food down our shirt fronts. My feet would be me.

But, as it is, up here is where I am, looking down over the hundred floors beneath me.

Or am I? Is this invisible processor behind my eyes really me?

A body often continues to live on after parts of the brain have died – even after what seems to be every consciousness-bearing aspect of it has failed – and we are inclined to continue treating it as the whole person it once was. But do we feel that a body that has *never* had a functioning brain, that was born without one, really constitutes a self? That it's a person? We don't know quite what to say. This is the puzzle at the heart of Peter Nichols's play, *A Day in the Death of Joe Egg*, where the father cannot feel that his brain-damaged child is a human being in any sense that makes a practical moral or social claim upon others, while the mother who actually brought it forth into the world cannot but.

Then again, I could lose quite a lot of my body and still feel I was me. In exceptional cases brains seem capable of supporting a sense of the self even when all possibility of expressing their function through perception and movement has gone. Or at any rate they seem capable of *continuing* to do so after the connection with the rest of the body has been lost. Can one imagine, though, that a brain could offer any sense of self or identity if it was the converse of Joe Egg's? If it had no body and sense organs to provide it with information? Had never had? If it had no memory of the possibility of physical expression?

This is what makes it so difficult to see how artificial intelligence can ever replicate animal intelligence. However you set up a system external to the body it can only do what it's been told to do, unless it can also feel for itself – unless it can suffer from doing this and take pleasure in doing that, unless it can experience the various urges that drive us as animals, to find fuel and to avoid danger, to survive and to reproduce ourselves before we wear out and cease to function; unless it can fear and desire. All these mechanisms were developed in us by the logic of evolution, because they give us a competitive edge over the inanimate and the insensate. And for all of them the services provided by the hundred lower floors are as essential as the department on the top floor that processes the information.

Here's what I'm starting to think, as I look down at my body and its history: that I'm the whole of me. That this body of mine isn't

246

something that simply belongs to me, the logistical support system for my brain – necessary, no doubt, but something external to the core of my real self. It *is* me, just as much as the belatedly curious head examining it. My identity runs through and through the structure, like 'Blackpool' through the rock, or the image through the hologram.

I suppose I've always known this. But there's a difference between knowing something without thinking about it (as one knows what country one's in, say) and knowing it consciously at this very moment, like a fresh discovery.

• • •

Still, when it comes to knowing something, which is what I'm trying to do with regard to my various scars and spots in this survey, then it's true that my brain is where the knowing is going on. What, with no ability to sense itself, does it know about its own adventures and malfunctions?

Well, some of its shortcomings are made manifest in performance. Mine has never really lived up to the character that the specs have seemed to suggest; I've usually been one of the least clever in any group I've been part of. Memory has always been a particular weakness – and now it's getting steadily worse. Each day, says Wikipedia, a hundred thousand brain cells die. So, in my thirty thousand days on earth, the best part of 3 billion have gone. Bearing off first of all people's names, followed by the names of places, books, plays, films and eventually everything else in the world.

Everyone has difficulties here, of course; names seem to be stored in a separate department from the rest of one's language, a room open to the elements on all sides, out of which the right names scatter like dead leaves in the autumn wind – and into which the wrong names sometimes drift to replace them. Numbers, too, are in some store where security is particularly lax. The PIN for my bank card, lodged so firmly most of the time that it enters itself on the little buttons in front of me without my thinking about it, sometimes turns out to have departed for a short holiday. The queue at the checkout waits while I look it up on my phone, where I keep it safely protected by a rather ingenious code . . . which turns out, as I stand there with everyone watching, to be away from its desk as well. Worse: the other day I turned on the radio and identified the Beethoven symphony they were playing, which was as familiar as the back of my hand, as the Fourth, when in fact it was the Third, which is totally different. Soon I shall be looking at the back of my hand itself and failing to know whether it's a hand or a foot.

Then I had an even odder and more disturbing episode. For half an hour or so my problem with names spread to the rest of the language – to common nouns as well as proper ones, to verbs, adjectives and adverbs. I was in a meeting about a professional matter and suddenly found to my dismay that I couldn't remember the words for what I wanted to say – or locate the meanings that should have been attached to the words that other people were uttering. It was as if English had suddenly become a foreign language, and one that I had only a very poor grasp of.

I was shaken. What had happened, I wondered afterwards when I'd got out of the meeting and normal service seemed to have been resumed. What had caused the problem?

Maybe there *wasn't* a cause, in any usual sense of the word, any more than there seems to be for biting my tongue. Perhaps the whole event was random. I'd got confused because . . . because I'd got confused. There have been many episodes in the course of my life when I've behaved in some odd and often embarrassing way for which I could later offer no explanation. Once – years ago, when I had about 2 billion more brain cells than I have now – I heard myself claim in the course of conversation to have been born in New York when in fact I was born in London, and do it not as a joke or an attempt to deceive but because I thought it was true. A few years ago, still with about 30 million more brain cells than now, I drove round a roundabout that I had used a thousand times before, and – not distracted, not day-dreaming, thinking about what I was doing – drove straight past the exit I meant to take. Scarcely able to believe what I'd done, and now concentrating even harder on getting it right, I continued round the roundabout to have another go – and found myself turning off two exits *before* the right one, so that I was heading back the way I'd come, in precisely the opposite direction to the way I wanted to go, and into an inescapable rush-hour jam.

Why did I do these things? I don't know. I just did them. They did themselves.

Maybe this is why I've spent so much of my life writing fiction. (Or maybe it isn't!) In fiction you can always ascribe causes to events. You can always know why your characters do what they do. Isn't this one of the purposes of fiction: to make sense of the world, to find the links between events that so often seem to be missing in real life? Just as authors are advised to limit themselves to no more than one coincidence per story, when real life (as Anthony Powell liked to point out) is full of coincidences, so any random events that do occur have to be remarked upon as exceptions to the causal rule: 'She would never know why she had happened to notice this one particular passer-by among so many others . . .'

But then, why had I fallen over in the bathroom? I hadn't tripped or slipped. I'd just . . . lost my balance. After all those years of keeping it. As I nursed my broken ribs next day, though, I recalled the meeting where English had become a foreign language, and it occurred to me with a sudden dismal certainty that these two apparently dissimilar events had something in common – that they both *did* have an identifiable cause, and that the cause was right here on the top floor of the building.

Which is why I made an appointment with the doctor.

• • •

In the course of the next week or two I had more contact with the NHS than I've had since it was founded, in the teeth of our then family doctor's opposition. First the four different GPs who happened to be available on the four different occasions I went to the surgery. Then two local hospitals, where between them I had two electrocardiograms, two brain scans, one arterial scan and a twenty-four-hour heart monitor. I gave specimens of my blood and my urine, and registered three different pulse rates and four different blood pressures. I was seen by a cardiologist, a neurologist and six radiologists, and I was prescribed three different sorts of pill.

I have to say I rather enjoyed most of it. There are a lot of amazingly nice people in the NHS. One of the two hospitals I went to had just been in the news, it's true, because a patient had starved to death unnoticed, but the prospects for outpatients like myself seemed to be rather more hopeful. Everything appeared to be clean. Everything was running on time. The paperwork flying back and forth between so many different departments occasionally went astray, but everyone was very friendly. The doctors explained patiently what they were going to do, and then what the result was. There was quite a lot of laughter, one way and another.

But yes, my guess was right: I'd had a small stroke. A so-called silent one, with no immediately detectable symptoms. It suggests, though, that I might have more – and perhaps in future ones that are not so quiet and self-effacing.

I'm dismayed, of course. Most of all to find that something I'd always taken so much for granted about myself, being fundamentally healthy, is no longer true. I've become one of the aged sick who are overburdening the health service and causing such problems to our fellow citizens. In the past I've always been a rather uninvolved member of the audience at organ recitals, as someone called the conversations that people of my age so often have, exchanging symptoms and comparing treatments. There was an evening not so long ago when everyone around the dinner table, some my age, some younger, compared notes on how many different sorts of pill they were now taking each day. I was a little embarrassed at the sparseness of my own tally: zero. Embarrassed but also, secretly, rather proud that I was costing the country so little. If you happen to be healthy it's difficult not to ascribe it privately to your own good sense and right thinking. Pride. I should have remembered what it goes before.

Falling over is a strikingly dramatic act. In an instant the world is transformed. Vertical has become horizontal. All possibility of forward motion has ceased. Well-washed hands and laundered clothes are in the dirt, perhaps splashed with blood which has seized its chance to break out of captivity. All your plans and intentions for the immediate future have vanished. You can't help being appalled at the sight of its happening, even to someone else. Or amused. Or, disturbingly, both. It's a simple physical metaphor for all the various ways in which human beings can lose the dignity they have acquired so painfully, and preserve so jealously, many of them far more subtly destructive to our social standing and our confidence in ourselves, few of them so immediately evident to both victim and audience.

For me, my own fall signified more than pride humbled; it also had something of the biblical connotation. I have lost my medical innocence. The gates of Eden are closed behind me, not by cherubim with a flaming sword, but by the big pharmaceutical companies with three different sorts of pill to be taken every evening for the rest of my life (with more varieties for the morning to come later!). One of them requires me to change my whole way of being; no more grapefruit! Grapefruit has been left behind like the fruit that made Adam and Eve as gods, knowing good and evil. I miss its tart deliciousness as much as they must have done the power of moral discrimination.

Yes, when I look down at those hundred floors below me now I see a building kept upright only by a dreary scaffolding of pharmacology. But then it was never quite as structurally sound as I thought, I realise now I've made this survey. It's like the countryside. So green and peaceful, as you look out over it on a summer's day. But a moment's thought and you realise that it's kept that way only by hard, underpaid agricultural labour, only by fertilisers and pesticides, only by bitter disputes in the local planning office. And every inch of it concealing a history of tribal conflict and civil wars, of Viking raids and rick-burnings, of brutal enclosures and foreclosures.

I suppose it's a hopeful lesson, on the whole, of how in time the grass will grow over almost anything. I should be grateful, in any case, to be alive when so many of my friends and contemporaries no longer are; to have had so little pain and handicap when others have had so much; and to have had those various pills invented and produced which will perhaps keep me going for a bit longer.

All the same, I can't help being a little dismayed, as I look out over the apparent peace of the now autumnal countryside, to find the greensward erupting and armed warriors rising from their graves to hack at each other once again.

· · ·

So, there's been some kind of raid on my already greatly depleted stock of brain cells. What had I been keeping in them? It's always difficult to identify an absence rather than a presence. Who's missing from your birthday party? What was in the desk drawer before the burglars came? You may not remember until months later, when you meet your absent guest in the street or at last need your little silver penknife. What am I missing in this case? All those names, of course, the genders of about thirty thousand German nouns, the things my wife says she's told me that I have no recollection of having heard. Most of them were probably gone or going years before this new break-in. Perhaps it was the identities of Beethoven symphonies. They were there until recently. Weren't they . . . ?

I was alarmed once again the other day when my wife pointed out, remarkably calmly, that I was driving on the right-hand side of the road instead of the left. We were in Berkshire at the time. Did I somehow think I was in the Lot-et-Garonne? I can't remember thinking anything in particular – or indeed thinking anything at all. I just did it. Mistakes like these, about knowledge so simple and so taken for granted, such as which country one's in, that one normally doesn't even think of it as knowledge, are particularly unsettling. Someone I know who is only a little older than me has taken to stopping at green lights and driving through red ones. We had another friend whose demented last days were overlaid by a mysterious stench in the sickroom, because, as his wife finally discovered, he had somehow forgotten the difference between a lavatory and a linen basket. Perhaps one of the things in that hole of mine was an ability that for eighty years I'd never even noticed I had: to stay upright in the dark.

The burglars are going to come back. Perhaps with sledgehammers this time, smashing down the front door and stripping the house in one massive organised assault. Or slipping quietly into empty rooms while my back's turned, taking a spoon here and a vase there, so that I never quite realise what's going on. There's a lot to take. My whole life, distributed around unmarked drawers, dumped in old grocery bags and dusty cupboards. Eighty years of accumulated possessions – my entire sense of being the person I am. Even if anything remains after the burglars have finished, it will be incinerated when the whole house is finally shut down.

This terminal brainlessness seems to me likely to cause problems to people who have made arrangements, as they believe, to 'inherit eternal life'. There's surely a bit of a contradiction in the doctrine, anyway. Christ himself was very specific about the qualifications for the bequest: you had to obey the Commandments, give all you possessed to the poor, and follow him. A great many of his supposed followers, however, have not only balked at the second condition but have insisted that if you fail the tests you're going to inherit eternal life anyway – be condemned to it, in fact, whether you like it or not, so that you can serve an eternal life sentence in some kind of divine penal institution.

Even if the contractual arrangements you made with such forethought and self-sacrifice have worked out as you hoped, though, and you get the long holiday you've paid the deposit on, problems surely remain. 'Welcome!' says the tour company's representative with genuine warmth when you arrive, her pen hovering over the list of eternitymakers. 'And you are . . . ?'

Yes – who are you? You've no idea. Names and all that kind of thing were stored in your brain, which is now reduced to ash and is fertilising a rose bush in some municipal garden of remembrance. 'No worries, pet!' says the rep. 'If you've forgotten your username or password all you need to do is answer these few simple questions. Mother's maiden name . . . ? Make of first car you owned . . . ?'

It's all gone, though. Everything you ever were, every trace of what makes you who you are. You can't even hear the questions, or see who's asking them, because your ears and eyes are under the rose bush with everything else. But at least you're not suddenly going to find your non-existent head down level with your non-existent feet, and suffer cracks in your non-existent ribs.

• • •

And yet I do believe in eternal life.

How long is eternity, after all? This a question with which cosmologists struggle – or give up as impossible to answer in scientific terms. Is it the lifespan of the universe in which we live, and which began, as we now believe, at one very specific moment 13-odd billion years ago? Or was there in some sense a time before this, in which nothing was? Or in which there were other universes? And before which there was – what? Still earlier universes? And will there be a time after it, they, end?

For me, though, and for you, the question is much simpler, because for each of us eternity is rather clearly defined. Time began for me when I was born and first brought the universe into being by reading shapes and similarities into it, by learning the identities and the attributes that others had allotted to them. Time and the universe will end for me when I close my eyes for the last time and the contents of my brain are cleared. I can project my imagination back, certainly, to what happened before I was born, and forwards to what will happen after I'm dead. But the life that I lend in this way to before and after lasts only as long as I have imagination to lend it. So for me my own lifespan and the lifespan of the universe are co-terminous, as yours and it are for you. When I die I shall have lived out my eternity. I shall have enjoyed eternal life, and when you die so will you.

Goethe:

Willst du ins Unendliche schreiten,
Geh nur im Endlichen nach allen Seiten.

Who in the infinite would go
Learn but the finite all around to know.

Yes, never mind the future perfect. The present tense is enough. I not only shall have enjoyed it – I am, and you are, enjoying it now. With as much of our brains and our senses as we can still muster.

• • •

So I shall never be dead. Not in *my* lifetime. I shall live and live and then . . . And then, yes, move seamlessly from the present tense to the future perfect: shall *have* lived, though I shall never know it. (Wittgenstein: 'Death is not an event in life.') What I shall have to find the courage to endure is not death but the approaches to it, which is likely to be test enough.

The deaths I do experience are the deaths of others. The longer I live myself the more of them there are. Bamber has died even since I began to write these remarks. The deaths of some of those still living are too painful to be contemplated – too unbearable to identify or be given the currency of words.

I'm thankful, though, that there is at any rate one person in the world considerate enough to spare my feelings. I shall never give myself cause for grief. Never shall I have to get out my well-worn black tie on my own behalf. Never shall I have to worry about who to ask to speak at my funeral, or how many people refreshments need to be provided for. No aching emptiness for me in the nights that follow. No guilt, or mean secret sneaking satisfaction, to have survived when someone else hasn't. It's other people who will suffer the pain and trouble. Let me take this opportunity to apologise to them all in advance.

So, eternal life. And yet . . .

And yet I can't help feeling a touch of sadness that eternity will end, even if I'm not here to experience it. A few scratches and breakages notwithstanding, a few griefs and desolations apart, this eighty-odd-year eternity of mine has been (as tour operators say) the journey of a lifetime.

• • •

All those tests and scans and electrodes, all that time expended by doctors and specialists, are justified by finding the traces of that stroke. But now here's the little ironic twist at the end of the story: whenever the stroke occurred, the neurologist doesn't think it was what caused the fall that set this whole investigation in motion. Nor, for that matter, the confusion with language that made me query the fall. It's pure coincidence. Two pure coincidences. One too many for any properly constructed story.

What did cause those two events, then? We shall never know, says the neurologist.

But if they hadn't happened the doctors wouldn't have looked for the cause. And if they hadn't looked for the cause they wouldn't have found the hole and prescribed the pills which may help to preserve me for a little longer yet.

• • •

So that was the happy ending to the story of my fall. Except that it wasn't an ending really, because time has passed since I wrote that last paragraph, and with it, unbelievably, first my eightieth birthday, and then nine more. Other troubles have come and gone. A few more falls, a few more pains to investigate. Another train of X-rays and scans, another televised visit to my intestines that I thought I should never see again. More electrodes attached to my chest, this time for longer; long enough to have detected an atrial fibrillation – an irregularity in my heartbeat that could encourage the formation of a clot in my blood, and raises the chances of another stroke, so the anticoagulant I was prescribed has been replaced by a stronger one. The three pills every evening have been joined by five every morning.

I suppose this is going to be the pattern of life from now on – more and more pains and malfunctions, more and more investigations, more and more pills. In the curiously muddle-headed way that life works, though, some things have got better instead of worse. One day in the middle of all these adventures, I became aware that I was feeling remarkably well – as well as I have ever felt in my entire life.

Another happy ending. Except that the very next day I was back in hospital for an emergency appendectomy.

But there it all is. For the moment. Me, from head to toe. So, while it lasts, a moment of celebration. Brain, I embrace you! Belly, heart, pancreas, those tiny feet down there – you, too! Scars, anomalies, malfunctions – the lot!

Or rather, we all together salute ourselves.

Acknowledgements

Some of these essays include material from previously published pieces by the author, including:

In 'Know-all', from an addition to the obituary of Eric Korn published in the *Independent* on 19 December 2014.

In 'Balloon from Saratov', from an addition to the obituary of Elizabeth Hill published in the *Guardian* in 1997.

In 'Berlin Blue', from the introduction to Sarah Haffner's memoirs, *Eine andere Farbe*, published in Germany by Transit Berlin in 2001. (The passage from Sarah Haffner herself comes from an essay in *Frayn in Germany*, edited by Susanne Bach and Albert-Reiner Glaap, published by Wissenschaftlicher Verlag Trier, 2008.)

In 'Five Minutes Fast', from the introduction to a reissue of John Gale's *Clean Young Englishman*, Hodder and Stoughton, 2015.

Wittgenstein quotations are from Ludwig Wittgenstein, *Tractatus Logico-philosophicus*, trans. D. F. Pears and B. F. McGuinness, Routledge & Kegan Paul, 1961.